Dedicated to all the *Renegades* with whom I've worked over
the years and all those who make their living in restaurants,
bars and hotels everywhere.

Your efforts define the *Renegade* spirit and demonstrate that,
although we may all do similar work, real success comes
in doing it in a way that is true to one's self.

When I waited tables and tended bar, a wise man once told me that
"You're only as good as your last happy customer."

I think that advice is as true for restaurant servers as it is for restaurant owners.

It's a fact that a *happy* guest spends more and comes back more often with their friends. So the question becomes: how do you make guests happy? And maybe an even better question is this: is a happy customer the result of a happy server or vice versa? I think that this insightful book by Tim Kirkland does a good job of answering those very questions and more, to the benefit of everyone who reads it.

Too many server manuals, books, DVDs, and training materials today seem to focus on one or two specific areas like service-giving or up-selling. Most of these materials tend to *talk down* to the server or bartender, offering rosy scenarios and perfect pitches that only make the waiter or waitress roll their eyes at the lack of realism or the writer's credibility. But Mr. Kirkland's holistic, fun, creative, and somewhat contrariant approach to 21st Century service, selling and customer connection reflects a new reality and refreshing approach for the iPod generation server, bartender and manager.

I wish I'd had this book when I began my career in foodservice, because it tells the truth and is chockablock full of creative tips, tricks and techniques that would have put a lot more cash in my pocket. I would have better understood how to take care of my guests, build business for the restaurant and increase repeat business every single shift. But my loss is your gain.

I know they say that *"money can't buy happiness,"* but every server and bartender I know says, *"Fork some over and watch me smile!"* Make better tips, have more fun, and learn how from A to Z in this valuable and long overdue book.

Read it and reap!

Jim Sullivan
CEO and Founder, Sullivision.com

Since the original publication of this book a few short years ago, a movement has been gaining momentum in the hospitality industry. Where once we spoke of customers we now speak of guests. Where once we measured Satisfaction, we now measure Experience. And many servers and bartenders have awakened to the fact that success is less about how we serve, and more about who we are, what we sell, and how we make people feel.

I've had the opportunity to speak with tens of thousands of servers, bartenders, managers and owners through my workshops and seminars. I've been fortunate to see the ideas in this book adopted, modified, used and improved to help front-line restaurant and bar teams make more money, create happier guests and more fulfilling work lives.

While the ideas and insights in this book are intrinsically effective, I've learned that they are most powerful when adapted to the unique personalities, capabilities and experiences of individual servers and their guests. This book is not about revealing an "Answer" or "Secret" to making more money. It's about evaluating how you work, amplifying strengths you already possess, and then leveraging your personality to greater service and sales success Growth. The truth is that Secret Knowledge or The One True Answer (or any such mythical list) will never make you more money. In fact, it's the mission of *The Renegade Server* to drive you away from the "one and only, tried-and-true" methods for making more money in the service industry. Instead we encourage you to find the things that are unique, genuine and relatable about yourself, and gain advantage by being who are.

Many hospitality employees believe that, once they have mastered the "Ten Terrific Steps of Service" or "Seven Stairs of Success" detailed in their employer's training materials, they have "arrived."

Truth is, you have <u>just</u> arrived.

Big-time monetary success does not come from *following the rules. Following the rules* is how you **keep** your job, not how you **excel** at it. Following the rules is how you work the POS. It's where you should put your coat, park your car, take your break and put stuff away. It's how to effectively and efficiently move plates and glasses from one room to another

True success does not come simply from *<u>following the rules</u>*. Never has.

Success comes from *mastering the rules* and then *building upon* them. Think about it.

The server you *love* is not the one who brings the plates/glasses out the quickest or who diligently spouts the script-of-the-day to your table. She is not the one who re-sets the table in the precise, prescribed arrangement or enters your food using the correct modifiers. The server you love (and TIP well) does something not detailed in the training manual. She connects with you. She makes it less about the food and more about the experience... the relationship. Sometimes — even if the food was late or wrong — you forgive it and come back for more. Not because of the food or the steps of service, but because of that *Renegade Server.*

I'd like to express my deepest gratitude to Jim Sullivan for his many vital contributions to this book and for his generous friendship and mentorship. Jim is universally recognized as the ultimate authority when it comes to training and motivating restaurant managers and crews. Many of the ideas put forward in this book regarding guest service can be further explored in his best-selling book, Fundamentals: *9 Ways to Be Brilliant at the Basics of Business,* in which I learned to lead like a "blowtorch" rather than a candle. That great advice continues to inspire me and countless others in this industry. His company, *Sullivision,* offers a wealth of restaurant and guest service resources on their website, **sullivision.com**.

I would also like to acknowledge the work of Dr. Michael Lynn of the Cornell University School of Hotel Administration. Dr. Lynn's immense body of work and research in the areas of social psychology and tipping behaviors have served as a tremendous resource and inspiration for this book. A collection of Dr. Lynn's findings and interpretations of various studies can be found in his e-book, *Megatips: Scientifically Tested Techniques to Increase Your Tips.* If you are interested in these behavioral findings, I highly recommend you download the booklet at **megatips.com**, and send a generous tip to Dr. Lynn.

Last, but certainly not least, I'd like to thank the many other servers, bartenders and restaurant managers I've been fortunate to meet and work with over the years, for lending me their experience and expertise and helping me keep the suggestions in these pages real.

Tim Kirkland
CEO and Founder, Renegade Hospitality Group
renegadehospitality.com

Servers: How to Get the Most from This Book!

Every valuable chapter defines certain challenges and truths about working in the modern restaurant environment as well as specific, immediately applicable techniques for dramatically increasing your tip income. To begin realizing these benefits right away, take advantage of the following:

1. Each chapter starts with a preview page that states the specific restaurant challenges addressed within. Take a moment to read these overview statements and determine how they compare with your own experience.

2. Each preview also lists the specific techniques that explain how to address those challenges. Consider what tricks and tools you already use to accomplish these "how to" steps.

3. Highlight the steps and techniques that appeal to you or may be especially appropriate for your restaurant. Apply them one or two at a time for several shifts, giving each your full consideration and attention. Note the differences in your tips or the way your guests react. Keep the ones that begin to feel comfortable and show results and lose those that don't fit.

4. Add a couple of techniques a week, building on your successes and gradually increasing your tips. Beware of hitting the floor with too many new approaches at a time, as it may dilute your execution of any one technique (and your success).

5. Each chapter contains various "Sidework" side bars designed to make you think about the way you currently work and interact with your customers. Contemplate these topics and discuss them with other servers.

6. At the end of each chapter, you will find a summary page which condenses the lessons and tools covered. Jot these review points down in your ticket book to help you focus on them during your shift.

Managers, Supervisors & Trainers

Share the money-making secrets of The Renegade Server with your entire team! By teaching everyone on your service staff how to increase their own income by...
- understanding how and why people tip
- making genuine, personal connections with their guests
- increasing their sales and guest satisfaction
- developing fiercely loyal regulars

...the restaurant wins and guests win, too!

1. Use the Chapter Previews to initiate discussions during training or pre-shift huddles about the current state of service in your restaurant and in the industry as a whole. Focus on how everyone may experience these challenges as a guest when they go out to other establishments.

2. Ask your team what tools and tactics they currently use to increase their tips. Look for ideas that align the interests of the server, the restaurant AND the guest. Create a special place to collect, share and save the freshest, best, and most appropriate ideas and credit the people who came up with them.

3. Ask members of your team to give an example of how they are hospitable in their everyday lives or homes, then have them convert that into an example of how they can display that hospitality in the restaurant.

4. Get your team members to write down instances they were extremely frustrated or delighted in a service situation outside of your restaurant. Discuss how the team can prevent those frustrating scenarios from creeping into your restaurant and how they can make the delightful experiences part of your restaurant's everyday service plan.

5. For more Leaders' guides, meeting ideas, discussions and incentives, check out the Extra Bonus section of ideas on how to *"Build a Renegade Restaurant"* at the back of this book.

6. Download the *"Renegade Server"* discussion guide at **renegadehospitality.com**

*Uncommon Strategies for Making More Money
in 21st Century Food Service*

"Why join the navy...
when you can be a pirate?"

Steve Jobs
Renegade CEO,
Apple, Inc.

Chapter 1:
Tip Theory

Preview

1. In recent years, there has been an explosion in the number of restaurants available to the average consumer.

2. This increase, along with time-stressed lifestyles, has led to a corresponding increase in the average number of times people go out to eat.

3. Because people are dining out far more often, and there are far more restaurants with similar offerings and service systems, dining out has become somewhat of a standardized **process** for many.

4. This standardization has also affected the reasons, amounts and ways which people tip.

5. **Today, most people do not base their tips on quality of service.**

6. In this chapter, you will learn what they **do** base their tips on, and what behaviors can affect that total tip number both upwards and downward.

How the changing perceptions of good service may be shrinking your tips.

Changing Perceptions of Service

The Clown changed everything. He was helped by the King, the Colonel and the little red-haired girl.

For countless years, the word "TIPS" has been accepted by those of us in the hospitality industry to be an acronym for:

T_o
I_{nsure}
P_{rompt}
S_{ervice}

Tips have grown to be an accepted and even *expected* part of dining out. Most Americans tip in an effort to encourage and reward efficient service, build goodwill for future visits, fulfill a perceived social obligation, or some combination thereof.

The United States has the highest restaurant tip expectation In the world at 15% - 20% of the total food and beverage bill.

Over the past few decades, however, quick-serve restaurant (QSR) operations like McDonald's and Burger King have changed the way Americans think about restaurant service.

How the changing perceptions of good service may be shrinking your tips.

Cleanliness and efficiency are the hallmarks of the quick-serve food industry. Through vision and rigorous training, these fast food mega-chains have virtually standardized a large portion of our collective dining experience. The Burger Boys and their pals have taught the American consumer that they can get:

- consistent food
- served piping hot
- in a timely manner
- in a clean environment
- for a reasonable price
- with a smile

In the early 1700's, brass urns inscribed "To Insure Promptitude" first appeared in British pubs and coffee houses.

The world's first tip jars.

All of that and no tip necessary!

Those QSR dining and service standards have become part of the American foodservice experience. Their standards of timeliness, efficiency, cleanliness and friendliness have set the bar for what is considered *acceptable* service.

Why would one consider *tipping* at a <u>full-service</u> restaurant for an experience that doesn't at least meet those minimum standards?

How the changing perceptions of good service may be shrinking your tips.

"To Insure Prompt Service?" These days, promptness (and the other basics that QSR's have made their stock-in-trade) is considered the *minimum "ante"* into the foodservice game!

If timeliness, cleanliness and friendliness only bring you to a guest's minimum "tip-worthy" expectations, then how can you catapult your tip income to the *next* level?

This book will show you why, in today's Casual Dining Culture, "TIPS" really means:

Check out this collection of awesome, creative tip jars at funnytipjars.com

T*reat Me Like a Regular*
I*ncrease My Check*
P*ersonalize My Service*
S*tand Out!*

In true *Renegade* fashion, however, we will take them out of order to better serve our immediate needs (hey... the road to success is not always straight... or even a road).

How the changing perceptions of good service may be shrinking your tips.

The Renegade Server

A *renegade* is loosely defined as one who breaks from tradition and commonly held beliefs. A *renegade* is a rebel, an outlaw.

The National Restaurant Association estimates that there are over 925,000 food service locations in America.

The Renegade Server is one who masters the basic training that everyone else is using, then adds his or her own unique service elements and guest connections in order to *stand out* and dramatically increase tips.

To become a *Renegade Server*, you must find ways to "up the ante" of basic restaurant service training.

With so many dining opportunities, it is becoming harder and harder to appear unique to the average consumer.

- *Build* upon the time-tested skills you've been taught by your employer.

- *Find* additional behaviors that shake your customers out of their fast-food service expectations.

- Turn the "*process*" of eating out into a *personalized experience*.

- Let each guest see you as a *real person* instead of just a "cog" in the restaurant machine.

- *Surprise* and *delight* every guest with unique service while connecting with them on a personal level and you will earn *stacks of money. Renegade-style. Guaranteed.*

How the changing perceptions of good service may be shrinking your tips.

The Casual & Family Giants

Casual Dining and Family Dining chains have become omnipresent in America. They represent those segments of the restaurant industry that provide full, tableside service, often including both dining room and bar.

Casual and Family Dining fill the gap between quick-serve (fast food) and fine dining. They serve a broad range of uses, from a full breakfast to a quick lunch, after-work happy hour or a birthday celebration dinner with friends.

They are our new neighborhood taverns and corner diners. From downtown to rural areas, Casual and Family Dining chains have become the cornerstone operations of the hospitality industry.

Chain operations now account for over 45% of all restaurants in America. Today, there is virtually nowhere you can go without seeing the familiar stripes of a T.G.I.Friday's awning or a trademarked red chili or neon apple hung over a restaurant

Most full-service restaurants can be categorized as either "Family Style" dining (those that do not offer alcoholic beverages) and "Casual Dining" (those that do).

How the changing perceptions of good service may be shrinking your tips.

door. For many communities, the appearance of an IHOP or Outback herald the town's *own* arrival on the map.

Casual and Family Dining restaurants have brought an accessible, affordable tableside restaurant experience into mainstream American life and helped increase the frequency of out-of-home dining by more than half.

Today in America, over 3 million people are employed by these restaurant chains, and each year over *$30 billion* is left behind for them in the form of gratuities.

To generate more tip income, you must find ways to make unique impressions on guests.

How much of that are you getting?
How much are you leaving in your guests' wallets?

Good Service

Imagine that tonight you go for dinner at your local casual dining bar and grill. You know the one. License plates, old-timey soda ads and used sports equipment nailed jauntily to the walls. On the table are large, colorful, absolutely *encyclopedic* menus featuring their *"world-famous"* burgers, or wings, or

How the changing perceptions of good service may be shrinking your tips.

blackened-chicken Caesar salad. There are little paper pup-tents that feature their *"X-plosive"* and *"X-treme"* appetizer popper-wraps as well as their *"patented"* signature cocktails.

You are greeted with a smile, and seated quickly. You are met by your server, who swiftly serves beverages and takes your dinner order.

Your server brings your order exactly as you ordered it. Nothing is wrong, and everything is on time.

The salads are served as the appetizer plates are cleared. Your entrées are piping hot and arrive as you take the last bite of salad. Within a couple of minutes, your server appears tableside and inquires as to your satisfaction with your meal.

Everything tastes great. Beverages are refilled as they empty, and the manager even stops by your table to check on the meal. After your plates are cleared, you are asked in a conspiratorial tone if you "saved room for dessert" and, upon declining, are promptly presented with your bill. Your charge slip is returned swiftly, and your server thanks you with a smile and invites you to return.

Most casual dining training is primarily designed to balance the needs of the guest and profitability of the restaurant.

It falls to you to add personal elements that help you drive your own income.

How the changing perceptions of good service may be shrinking your tips.

Many restaurant trainees think that once they have mastered the technical steps in their restaurant's training program they "have arrived." Truth is... they have only "just arrived." It's the personal touches you layer on TOP of the technical training that truly deliver success!

This experience, plus or minus some degree of pre-scripted "salesmanship" is generally accepted to be the basic model of good service in a casual dining setting. It has been engineered to meet the common expectation of good service, maximize check average and keep the traffic flow in the dining room (turns) moving. It is, indeed, a model for good service and, if followed, will earn at least average tips.

The Renegade Server knows that it is only the very beginning of how to make huge, amazing tips! To break away from earning an average income, you must distinguish yourself against the background of common service. Read on. This book will show you how.

Amazing Tips

Think about the last time you left a really, *really* extravagant tip in a restaurant. Has there ever been a time when you have been so moved or excited by the service that you bothered to speak to a manager or even write a letter or email? What was it that left you so impressed and wanting to go "above and beyond" in rewarding your server?

How the changing perceptions of good service may be shrinking your tips.

Chances are the situation or actions that left you so impressed had little or nothing to do with the quality of food, beverage or "steps of service." In all likelihood, the thing that knocked off your socks was something unusual and not detailed in that restaurant's training program. Did you encounter some kind of problem that was gracefully handled by your server? Did your server go out of her way to find you something special or to accommodate a request?

Really amazing experiences (*and tips*) generally arise from situations that *stand out*. By learning how to identify and take advantage of those opportunities and situations, you will become a *Renegade Server*.

Restaurants often train their service staffs to deliver a repeatable experience that **meets** the average guest's expectations.

That means that they train all of their servers to deliver some version of the *same experience to each guest, every time.*

If you have worked for more than one restaurant in your life, what are the "transferable skills" that are trained in all?

What are the skills and habits you bring with you?

_____

_____

_____

_____

_____

_____

_____

_____

_____

_____

How the changing perceptions of good service may be shrinking your tips.

This training philosophy benefits the restaurant in that it delivers a level of friendly consistency that satisfies the vast majority of their guests.

As a server, you are trained to approach every dining transaction with the same "steps of service" that your employer has found to be effective in serving the maximum number of guests to their satisfaction.

"Because, sometimes it's just boring hitting a normal golf shot"

- Tiger Woods
Renegade Golfer

Try to remember your training upon being hired. Chances are your experience covered some or all of these points:

- **Steps of Service:** timing, order and mechanics of serving food correctly (greeting, then beverage, then appetizer, etc.).

- **Salesmanship:** prescribed sales "pitches" and "approaches" designed to maximize the guests' spending while in the restaurant: "up-selling," and "suggestive-selling."

- **Basics & Mechanics:** "where is it, what should it look like, how do I ring it up, what do I wear, when do I work, when do I get paid..."

This training will definitely provide you with a good start towards a happy work environment and good

How the changing perceptions of good service may be shrinking your tips.

tips. If, however, you want to turn "good tips" into AWESOME, HUGE or AMAZING tips, you must find ways to make an impression on your guests **between** your perfectly executed "Steps of Service."

You have to find ways to stand out and make a unique impact. It is by finding these additional opportunities that you will make a special connection with your guests and exceed their expectations of the casual dining experience.

Tip Theory

In order to figure out how to dramatically boost tip income, one should first have a thorough understanding of how and why people tip. A great way to figure that out is to observe people who are successful at earning big tips.

Every restaurant has some servers that make tons of tips, and some who barely get by. Same restaurant, same food, same guests... the difference could only be the servers themselves.

In my years as a server, bartender, restaurant

"If you work just for money, you'll never make it... But if you love what you're doing, and you always put the customer first, success will be yours."

- Ray Kroc,
Renegade Milkshake Salesman (and Founder of McDonald's)

How the changing perceptions of good service may be shrinking your tips.

manager and owner, I noticed that the servers who stayed around the longest and worked the hardest were also those who were making the most money. I also noticed that those who didn't make great tips sooner or later left in search of a place where they might "make better money."

While it's easy to assume that the people who made more money did so because they stuck around longer and worked harder, it's really a chicken-or-the-egg question.

"It is not enough to give the Customer good service. You must subtly make him aware of the great service he is getting."

- Unknown

Isn't it possible that they actually stuck around and worked harder *because* they were making great money, and didn't want to leave a good thing?

Furthermore, isn't it *equally* possible that it was not the "place" that dictated how much money they could make, but the servers *themselves*?

I decided that if I wanted to stack my staff with hard-working, long-term players, I should simply try to *find and hire those people that had already figured out how to make great money.*

So I started asking every interviewee the same question…

How the changing perceptions of good service may be shrinking your tips.

> *"What's the best way you know to <u>increase</u>*
> *your tips in a restaurant?"*

I figured the superstars I was looking for would have the right answers. I thought by asking "the money question," I'd be able to find those servers that had already figured out the secrets to good customer service. My results were mixed, but the answers I received were always educational.

When I started training and consulting for corporate restaurants, I continued to begin every seminar and workshop with the same question:

> *"What's the best way you know to <u>increase</u>*
> *your tips in a restaurant?"*

For your education and information, I have taken the liberty of writing down the top answers I heard every time, hundreds of times.** Drum roll please...

Research shows that individual gratuities are less driven by the desire to incentivize good service, and more driven by factors such as status and check total.

Dubious "Fact" #1 –
The 10 Best Ways to Increase Tips:

1. Smile
2. Be friendly
3. Be 'genuine'

**NOTE (Do not stop reading after this list... *these are not the real secrets of this book!!)*

How the changing perceptions of good service may be shrinking your tips.

4. Make sure to 'get it right' (their food & drink orders)
5. Make the service quick and efficient
6. Remember what the guest is drinking
7. Keep cups / glasses refilled
8. Don't keep the guest waiting
9. Be engaging
10. Say *"Thank You"*

Recently, certain New York City restaurants abandoned the customary guest driven gratuity system in favor of a standard "service charge" added to the bill.

The fact is, everyone *knows* the tactics above are common sense to the good server. These are the "ante" into the game… the "greens fees" of playing for tips. The list above practically defines the *basics* of good service… yet so many identify them as being special tactics for *improving* tips.

Some servers left in protest, citing that they felt the set charge would actually reduce their income, as they often inspired more grand gestures of generosity from their guests.

And good service is what people tip for.
Right? Maybe not. Read on…

Dubious "Fact" #2 –
People Tip for Good Service

Have you seen those television commercials for the bed that you can customize to the precise level of firmness or softness you desire? You see the spokesperson lying on this beautiful mattress, extolling the life-changing benefits of finding one's "sleep number"?

How the changing perceptions of good service may be shrinking your tips.

Those ads have made me think. I have a personal *"Tip Number"* where I'm always comfortable, too. I think everyone does.

Think about it. How do you usually determine your tip? If you're like most people, you begin by looking at the check total and applying a percentage amount. This percentage is applied reflexively, every time. That's your "Tip Number."

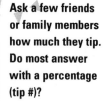

Ask a few friends or family members how much they tip. Do most answer with a percentage (tip #)?

How many simply reply "it depends on the service?"

My Tip Number is 20. That means that my first step in determining a tip is to figure out 20% of the total of the check…

TIP NUMBER | **% of Total Check Amount**

Today, most people would say their Tip # is between 15 and 20. If you are in the hospitality industry, chances are your Tip # is between 20 and 25. What's your parents' Tip #? Probably around 15% (unless you have them better trained). Your grandparents?

Probably as low as 10%.

How the changing perceptions of good service may be shrinking your tips.

Occasionally, every server even sees some guy who is *so devoted* to his *odd* Tip # that he actually carries around a little chart in his wallet that helps calculate the percentage he should leave behind.

Think again about your Tip #. Do you consider it a "good tip"? Of course you do. You wouldn't leave it if you didn't. You're not *cheap!* What about your parents or grandparents? Even though their Tip # is likely lower than yours, do they believe it to be a fair tip? They sure do. *No one* wants to think of themselves as cheap.

Most of the 'tricks' and behaviors that servers believe will earn them more tip money are already expected by the guest, and therefore will only get them to a guest's average tip level.

Now… does your good tip include friendly, timely service? Do you expect a genuinely engaged server that gets your order right and remembers what you are drinking?

For your **20% base tip**, don't you expect your waiter to be gracious, smile at you and say '*thank you*' when you're finished?

In essence, all of the behaviors listed in Dubious *"Fact" #1* (smile, be friendly, be genuine, get it right, keep drinks refilled, say thank you, etc.) are actually already included <u>and</u> <u>expected</u> in your Tip #.

How the changing perceptions of good service may be shrinking your tips.

That means that all of the tactics many servers believe are making them more and better tips are actually just the ante into the game!

You have to do all of those things to get to the basic Tip # (which is really based on the check total, anyway)... you don't get extra credit for them.

So, in reality, *"Fact" #2* (people tip for good service) is also false, or at least overstated. People don't base their tip on service. **They base it on their check total; with an _expectation_ of good service**.

> "The man who waits for a roast duck to fly into his mouth must wait for a very long time."
>
> - Asian Proverb

Remember, the Tip # is just the first step in the tipping ritual. The important thing to notice here is that the first thing people base tip totals on is *percentage of the check total.*

"My Tip #" is not based on the quality of service (that comes later).

Research indicates that check total, not service, is the strongest influencer of tips. In fact, it is stronger than all other factors combined.

How the changing perceptions of good service may be shrinking your tips.

Think of that the next time you are wondering if it is really in your interest to sell that special dessert.

How Bigger Tips Are *Really* Made

Increasing your tips is simple. If people primarily, automatically figure tips based on check total, your choices include:

1. Present the largest check total possible *(increase sales volume)*.
2. Present as many checks as you can *(create devoted regulars)*.
3. Find other, small ways to inspire generosity above and beyond the guest's "Tip #" *(stand out & impress with hospitality)*.

The following chapters are each devoted to showing you simple, immediate ways to accomplish each of these goals.

"Life is a game. Money is how we keep score."

- Ted Turner
Renegade Billionaire

Building on My Tip

It's very difficult to move people off of their Tip # (when was the last time you thought, *"She was a great server... I think I'll go up to 23 percent."?)*

How the changing perceptions of good service may be shrinking your tips.

People do, however, leave bigger tips. Just not by percentage.

If things go very, very right (or very, very wrong), people adjust their tip up or down depending on unique experiences.

Most research indicates that people add to and subtract from their Tip # incrementally by dollars and cents. In other words; if I loved your service, I would figure out my usual 20% and then throw in an extra buck or two (or round up to the next $5 or $10). Same deal for bad service... except I'd adjust downward.

It doesn't take a genius to figure out that those incremental movements from the check-based percentage go up for certain behaviors and down for others.

The greatest time-related Guest frustrations are usually expressed relative to the service of other guests... such as the perception of being seated or served out of chronological order.

+$

PERSONALITY

TIP NUMBER

% of Total Check Amount

Many studies show that most *positive* incremental tip additions come from issues related to the personality of the server. In order to feel that positive personality "vibe," you must make a personal connection with the guest and be

How the changing perceptions of good service may be shrinking your tips.

recognized as an individual. That's what being a *Renegade Server* is all about.

TIP NUMBER

TIME

- $

% of Total Check Amount

Furthermore, it has been noted that most *downward* tip increments are caused by issues related to time. Slow service, late food, and infrequent check-backs are chief among restaurant service complaints and are the primary reasons guests 'ding' your tip.

Remember that in order to make more money, you must not just figure out how to make tips go up; *but also how to stop tips from going down.*

This book will help you increase your tip income exponentially by sharing creative ways to:

- Increase the check totals on which you are primarily tipped.
- Increase your check & customer counts by developing devoted regulars.
- Make personal connections with guests and stand out as an individual.
- Rescue your tips in situations where your guests are focused on time.

How the changing perceptions of good service may be shrinking your tips.

We'll share time-tested, scientifically proven techniques that will help you to stand out in the restaurant business.

By making these behaviors part of your new routine, you will learn to present yourself as an *individual* to your guests. By doing so, you will experience the **explosive growth of your tips**.

Find out how to keep your tips from going down by learning how (and how not) to handle mistakes and guest complaints. Check out the "Quick Tips" bonus section at the back of this book.

What the Icons Mean:

Watch for specific techniques you can use to increase your tips marked this icon.

Actual scientific research that you can use to make more money is marked with this icon.

Sometimes, it is just as important to know what NOT to do. Look for this icon to help you avoid a misstep or "pit" (literally, the opposite of a "tip").

How the changing perceptions of good service may be shrinking your tips.

Most importantly, you will learn to make real, personal connections with your guests by breaking away from the language that is used in every other restaurant in North America. We will mark those over-used phrases with this icon.

Finally, learn to use language that truly endears you to your guests and inspires them to tip you more. It is marked with this icon.

GUEST CHECK

2 Iced Tea	1.99
	1.99
2 Diet Cola	1.99
	1.99
Chix Caes	10.49
Burg/Fries	8.99
Ribs	13.49
Chix Pasta	12.29
tax	3.87
	57.09

Periodically throughout *The Renegade Server,* we will review the techniques discussed and assess their value to your income by re-visiting a typical guest check.

How the changing perceptions of good service may be shrinking your tips

SUMMARY

1. *Most people make their tip decision by looking at the total amount of the check, and applying a standard percentage; their "Tip #."*

2. *Most peoples' "Tip Number" already includes those things we consider perfect service (smiling, friendliness, quickness…).*

3. *Guests often adjust their Tip Number up in dollar increments based on "personality" or the impression the server made upon them.*

4. *Guests often adjust their Tip Number down in dollar increments based on issues related to time.*

5. *To dramatically increase tips, servers should concentrate on:*

   • Increasing the check total on which they are tipped.

   • Increase the number of checks they deliver by creating regular, frequent customers.

   • Make personal connections with their guests.

Chapter 2:
Personalize My Service

Preview

1. In today's world, restaurants don't just sell food and drinks... they sell **experiences**.

2. Your success as a server depends on your ability to successfully determine, deliver and surpass the unique experience your guest is expecting.

3. Each guest's **expectations** are different, and depend on a variety of factors.

4. In this chapter, you will learn how to observe and connect with each guest and determine exactly what those expectations are via:

   - How often (if ever) they've been in your restaurant.
   - Why they are in your restaurant.
   - What they are likely to buy.
   - How they want their experience to be paced and how much time they have.

5. Last, you will learn specific techniques that will allow you to exceed each of those unique expectations, delighting your guests and exploding your tips.

People don't go out to restaurants to eat.

Newsflash:

People don't go out to restaurants to eat.
They don't go out to bars to drink.

For most people, both eating and drinking can be done quicker, easier, cheaper, often better and even safer in the comfort of their own homes. Think of the best, biggest, most important meals of your life… your annual Thanksgiving feast, perhaps… usually done in the home.

Yes, I grant you, people *eat in restaurants* and *drink in bars*. But those aren't the reasons that they go. What are the reasons? I don't know. Neither do you. Nor does the CEO of the restaurant company you work for.

For us, it may be "just another meal," but for our guests it is _always_ an occasion.

The fact is that people go out to restaurants for many, many different reasons. Every table you serve this week is sitting in your restaurant for a different reason… and *expecting a different experience.*

When approaching your business (your section),

People don't go out to restaurants to eat.

always remember that people go out for their *own* reasons, not for ours.

Starbucks' legendary service philosophy:

Connect.
Discover.
Respond.

It is far too easy to slip into the day-to-day mindset that guests are in our restaurants simply to sit down, order food, eat it, pay, *tip* and leave.

Sure, all of these steps speak to the <u>process</u> that has become casual dining… but it is that same process that has stuck nearly every server in America in a tip rut.

Food and drink are the <u>*what*</u>. To become a *Renegade Server* – and make more money – you must figure out the <u>*why*</u>.

Have It Your Way

These days, everything is customized for individuality. There are *thousands* of ways to personalize an order for coffee at Starbucks. We buy computers custom-built to serve our own unique interests and needs. Our phones are loaded with personal settings, playlists and apps that uniquely suit our preferences and needs. Our golf clubs, skis and

People don't go out to restaurants to eat.

running shoes are conformed to our body, style and skill. Even our burritos and sub sandwiches are made to our particular, exacting specifications while we watch.

Our world has gone custom.

The dining experience is no exception. You must approach every table with the knowledge that your guests are here for a particular reason (and therefore a particular experience) that only they know.

"The first step in exceeding your customers expectations is to know those expectations."

- Roy H. Williams

It is the *Renegade Server's* job to find out what those reasons are and cater to the guests' unique expectations.

Imagine how much more tip money you will make if you can deliver a personalized experience that pinpoints and exceeds each of your guests' secret expectations (instead of simply going through the *process* performed by every other server in the business).

Consider the different dine-out reasons, and therefore the very different priorities and expectations, of the following tables:

People don't go out to restaurants to eat.

How do your own dining and service expectations change depending on who you are with and why you are out?

1. A couple of young twenty-somethings on their first date.

2. Three factory-working guys, just off a double shift.

3. Six middle-aged soccer moms together for "Girls' Night Out".

4. A young married couple and their three kids, all under the age of 6

5. Four college students in to watch "the big game."

6. A visitor in from out of town, staying at the hotel down the street

7. Four young couples, one of which has just gotten engaged.

8. Two men in business attire in for lunch.

9. Four Senior Citizens at breakfast.

Clearly, all of these table scenarios represent wildly different reasons for being in a restaurant.

It is possible, however, for many of these tables to be in the same restaurant at the same time! Even in the same *section*.

People don't go out to restaurants to eat.

If all of these tables have different reasons for being in a restaurant, doesn't it stand to reason that they all have different expectations of their experiences?

If you knew about all of those different expectations, wouldn't you want to "flex" your service style to accommodate each group of guests in order to make a better tip?

To be a *Renegade Server*, you must become a master at figuring out what the guest expects, then delivering it with abundance.

Personalize your guest's experience by learning little ways to show care for them in the Quick Tips section in the back of this book.

The simple, boring "food-fetcher" server approaches each table with the same style, attitude and skills – and reaps average or below tips. Meanwhile, the *Renegades* are attracting more big-tipping "whales" and developing a regular clientele that will increase their incomes exponentially.

In order to personalize each guest's experience, you should determine and use these four "R's" at each and every table:

People don't go out to restaurants to eat.

 Recon

 Regularity

 Reason

Rate

You've just been seated with a one top... a single woman in a business suit. Try to imagine what brings her in today. What are some things that might tip you off?

_____
_____
_____
_____
_____
_____
_____
_____
_____

Recon (short for *reconnaissance*) is a military term for surveying a situation in order to gain information for strategic purposes. Generals in the field use *recon* in order to make and revise plans and get maximum impact. You should do the same in your section.

With each new table, don't simply walk up and begin going through the "motions" of your steps of service. Take a moment to *recon* the table. Look closely at your new guests, and make a few quick decisions based on what you see. This is an important step to becoming a *Renegade Server*, because it is <u>this</u> information that will allow you to personalize your table approach.

People don't go out to restaurants to eat.

In addition to how many people are seated at the table, make note of how they are dressed, their ages, genders, and the general make-up and demeanor of the group. Take a second to notice additional items on or around the table.

"You can observe a lot just by watching."

- Yogi Berra
Renegade Baseball Player & Manager

Are they dressed up, or are they wearing football jerseys?

Are they accompanied by children?

Do they have gifts, cards, or shopping bags at the table?

Do they appear to be rushed or hurried?

Have they reserved or requested special seating?

How do they interact? Like family, friends, romantics or business associates?

What is their energy level? Are they upbeat? Serious?

People don't go out to restaurants to eat.

"Read" your guests, but don't stereotype them.

Just take a moment before you approach the table and make a mental snapshot of the group or individual.

Form an educated guess as to what they may be expecting from this restaurant experience.

Now, customize your approach and decide how you will greet them, how you will change your service style and what you will sell to them in order to meet those unique expectations.

Using our sample scenarios, what are some visual cues that you can *recon* from these guests, and begin personalizing their service?

1. **A couple of twenty-somethings on their first date.**

   • may be dressed up (more than other guests).
   • perhaps they are displaying nervous body language.

2. **Three factory working guys, just off a double shift.**

   • wearing the same uniform, jackets.
   • carrying tools or equipment.

3. **Six middle-aged soccer moms together for a "Girls' Night Out."**

   • may be dressed up.

People don't go out to restaurants to eat.

- is there a "guest of honor?"
- no kids, husbands or boyfriends

4. A young married couple and their three kids all under the age of 6.

   - kids, high chairs, strollers, etc.

5. Four college students in to watch "the big game."

   - are they wearing a particular team attire?
   - what is their energy level?

6. A visitor in from out of town, staying at the hotel down the street.

   - guests dining alone often bring work or reading materials.
   - is this guest looking around as if it's her first time here?

Focus on the guest and why they are in your restaurant. Be interest*ed* before being interest*ing*.

Knowledge speaks, but wisdom listens.

7. Four young couples, one of which has just gotten engaged.

   - are there gifts, cards or balloons at the table?
   - who are the guests of honor?

8. Two men in business attire in for lunch.

   - is there paperwork on the table?
   - is this a working lunch, or a break from work?

9. Four Senior Citizens in for breakfast.

   - is this an "after church" breakfast?
   - do they have special needs or seating requirements?

People don't go out to restaurants to eat.

By taking a moment to observe your table, you can begin to plan your first approach, adapt your service style based on what you see, and decide what items they are likely to desire.

What is special or different about your restaurant that first-time guests would need or want to know?

_____

_____

_____

_____

_____

_____

_____

Regularity ... determine how often they visit your restaurant. Are they regulars, or is it their first time in? Is there anything about your restaurant that a first time guest may need or like to know? If a guest dines at your restaurant frequently, what are they looking for from their experience?

I recommend that you begin every guest interaction by finding out how often, if ever, they have visited your restaurant. Make it part of your first approach. Asking guests if they have been in before or if it is their first time will allow you to put the first time visitor at ease with guidance, while honoring regular customers (*"You've been here before, right? No?! Then welcome!"*).

Consider the unique needs and expectations of new visitors versus regulars:

People don't go out to restaurants to eat.

First Timers | *Regulars*

First Timers	Regulars
May be looking for that special dish for which your restaurant is famous.	Are more likely looking for what's new or special on the menu.
Tell them what's popular with staff and regulars.	Point out seasonal items or limited time offers.
Will need to know a little about the restaurant (or the location of the restrooms).	May have a favorite seat or server for whom they are looking.
Should be introduced.	Should be recognized.

Always ask yourself: "Is this decision guest-focused or server-focused?"

Asking Guests if it is their first visit leads you into natural conversations about whatever it is you want to sell or recommend.

"Have you ever been here before? No? Well, we're famous for our homemade pies and pastries, so make sure to check out our pie menu."

"Have you ever been here before? You have? Great. What's your favorite pie? I like the blueberry, too, but make sure to check out the new cream pies we added last week!

People don't go out to restaurants to eat.

**The "first visit" question always
leads naturally to the products
you want to talk about.**

Reason... Use your "recon," as well as any additional information you get from your guests to determine why they came in to this particular restaurant on this particular night.

Why people are in a restaurant has a profound effect on what they expect from their server, as well as what they are likely to buy.

Never say you "ran out" of a special. Say you "sold out" and offer an alternative entrée that's equally as enticing.

Think again about our guest scenarios, and add your own thoughts about what unique experience they may be expecting. Think about what types of products they are most likely to buy.

1. **A couple of twenty-somethings on their first date.**

   • This couple would probably like to focus on getting to know one another. That means you should try to keep table interruptions to a minimum. Don't approach when they are looking directly at each other... wait until they are looking around or down.

People don't go out to restaurants to eat.

- Try to make them look <u>good</u> in front of each other. Reinforce their orders by saying things like "excellent choice," and "that's one of our best items." Never belittle, correct or unintentionally embarrass them. If they mispronounce a menu item, you should write it down and let it slide... they care more about looking good than using the correct pronunciation of foie gras.

- Offer the wine list, and recommend a <u>bottle</u> of wine. Buying a bottle of wine is a great way for someone to look knowledgeable and show that he (or she) is not afraid to drop a little cash. It also makes sure they both get two glasses of wine... which never hurts when coping with first-date nerves.

- Try to discern ahead of time who is hosting. Use that information to make taking care of the check as smooth as possible, keeping the awkwardness of check-wrangling to a minimum.

- Think before you suggest. You may not be successful suggestively selling items that are messy or that could impart bad breath to first daters.

Think again of your one-top, single lady. What might be the "Reason" for her visit? Considering that reason, what would you recommend to her?

_____
_____
_____
_____
_____
_____
_____
_____

2. Three factory working guys, just off a double shift.

People don't go out to restaurants to eat.

- The obvious choice for these guys is beer… and keep it coming 'til they quit complaining about their boss.

- Consider that their happy hour with each other might accidentally spill over into the dinner hour at home. Recommend they order full dinners to take home with them. In my experience, if you are coming home late from work and smelling like beer… it helps to show up with a great meal from a full-service restaurant in hand!

Take a moment to decide how you will approach and serve each new table.

3. Six middle-aged soccer-moms together for a "Girls' Night Out."

- All dressed up with no husbands or kids in tow? Suggest fancy cocktails, like cosmopolitans… or any other drink featured on *Sex & the City*.

- Girls' Night Out is all about luxury and decadence (whereas Guy's Night is often about partying). Suggest exotic, shareable appetizers or tapas. Offer to bring a lot of small things that can be used as "centerpiece" items for everyone to share while they catch up with each other.

- While it has been my experience that ladies can sometimes be very conservative about dessert purchases, Girls' Night is time for indulgence. Offer to bring out a few desserts, pile them up in

People don't go out to restaurants to eat.

the middle of the table, and make sure to pass out plenty of forks!

4. **A young, married couple and their three kids all under the age of 6.**

   - This family is probably focused on getting in, getting the kids fed, and getting out before anything gets broken. Timing is a main consideration.

   - Obviously, kids' menus and any other kid-friendly accessories should be offered (such as crayons, crackers and toys).

   - Many parents prefer milk and juice be offered to their kids, rather than soda – which is a win for you, too, since these items often cost a little more, and are seldom refillable. If possible, always serve kids' beverages in cups with lids.

   The Server's Law:
   "If I take the
   money, I will do
   the work"

   - Tim Hansen

   - Address and engage the kids directly and by name, if possible. If you can engage the tots and allow the parents a few moments of stolen peace so they can eat, they will reward you handsomely.

   - Kids are primary drivers of family restaurant choice. Make sure the kids know your name, so that they will ask to come back and sit in <u>your</u> section.

People don't go out to restaurants to eat.

5. Four college students in to watch "the big game."

   - For this group, the game is the primary reason to be out. They are just in your restaurant so they can watch the game in close proximity to nachos and beer. Make sure to offer shareable snacks.

   - Be aware of the game. When your team (or the team for which your guests are rooting) scores, you should know it. A well-timed suggestion of a "touchdown" or "goal" shot will result in much better sales… <u>but you have to know when your team scores</u>.

   - Make sure these guests have a good view of the TV sets and have plenty of access to other sports fans. The camaraderie between fans (even for opposite teams) results in longer stays and higher sales. Introduce them to each other.

Earning customer trust is the first step to earning customer tips.

One of the best ways to establish trust is with a prompt and friendly greeting.

6. A visitor in from out of town, staying at the hotel down the street.

   - Anyone having a meal alone is obviously susceptible to a little boredom. Upon confirming that the guest is not expecting anyone to join later, offer a newspaper or magazine (and make sure they have enough light by which to read it).

People don't go out to restaurants to eat.

- If the person is dining in the bar or lounge area, make sure to introduce him or her to a couple of regulars or to the bartender. More than once, a *Renegade* has turned the sale of one beer into three or four by getting a new guest into a spirited conversation with a regular and extending their stay. That's multiplying the tip by 300%-400%!

- People from out of town are tourists (even if they're here on business). Make sure they get to hear all about what you're <u>famous</u> for, so they feel like they got the <u>real</u> (insert city name here) <u>experience</u>. You know, crab cakes in Maryland, steaks in Omaha, lobsters in Maine, mojitos in Miami, etc...

- Guests who are visiting your city may want a souvenir to remind them of their trip. Suggest t-shirts, glassware or other merchandise that have the names of your restaurant and city on them. Most often, guests tip on the check total including these items, not just food and beverage. That's an additional commission on merchandise!

The answer is "yes"...

Now what's the question?

People don't go out to restaurants to eat.

7. **Four young couples, one of which has just gotten engaged.**

    - This group is out to celebrate. It is for <u>this</u> table that your restaurant carries that bottle of champagne or sparkling wine. Offer to chill it before dinner, and make a big display of opening it.

    - People who have just gotten engaged have a busy year ahead of them. They will be throwing many parties, hosting tons of out-of-town friends and relatives, and having showers and rehearsal dinners. Those people and parties will need food and drinks. Make sure the bride-to-be has your restaurant's take-out menu, large party information and banquet manager's card. Most of all make sure she has your name, and knows to ask for you when booking all of these big-ticket, big-gratuity events.

    For ideas on how to acknowledge your guests' birthday celebrations, check out the Quick Tips section in the back of this book.

    - Ask frequently if the group would like you to take photos of them with their cameras. You have to ask first... it doesn't count if they have to ask you.

8. **Two men in business attire for lunch.**

    - If paperwork or laptops are on the table, they are looking for "invisible service." Be quick, attentive, quiet and efficient. Ask if they have specific time constraints. Make recommendations as you place

People don't go out to restaurants to eat.

the menus down... as their lunch decision is not the decision they came here to make.

- They will take a long time to decide. Offer to bring them a cup of soup or a tidy (no sauces), shareable appetizer as a "center-piece" to pick at while they take their time with their menus. They may tell you a couple of times that they "haven't even looked" at the menu, so it's your job to get items on the table, and to make suggestions.

- Once they have their food and drinks, go into stealth mode. Automatically refill waters, teas and coffees without interrupting to ask if they need refills. The same goes for empty plates... just take them away, don't ask if they're finished with them. Don't avoid them just because you don't want to interrupt them! It may slow service, and this table is likely on a timeline.

- Silently change out their beverage napkins or coasters about every 10 minutes. This method is used to get repeat drink orders. When you grab a glass in order to switch out a dry coaster, the guest will naturally look at you. Use this brief, silent break to sell the next drink without "interrupting" their conversation.

When dealing with people, remember that you are dealing with creatures of emotion, not logic.

People don't go out to restaurants to eat.

9. Four Senior Citizens in for breakfast.

    *   For retired persons, this may be a social meal, rather than a quick breakfast on the way to the office. Adjust your service style to keep their cups full while being unobtrusive enough to allow for conversation.

Rate... Research (and probably your own experience) has shown that most guest complaints and other factors that can damage your tip have to do with time.

No one who gives his best ever lives to regret it.

When deciding whether to alter their usual tip (Tip #) up or down based on their experience, most guests first consider how long things took compared to their expectations. Guests can be especially critical about how long it takes to place their orders, receive their food or drinks, and even pay their checks.

Often, guests rate their service based on the rate of service for other guests around them.

How many times have you heard *"that table was seated after us, but they're **already** eating and we're not!!"*?

People don't go out to restaurants to eat.

We know that guests' timing expectations are a primary influencer of tips and that each guest's experience expectations are unique. Doesn't it stand to reason that your guests' expected *rate* of service is closely tied to the *reason* they came in?

Once again, let's look at our various guest scenarios. How might the guests' expectations regarding the rate of service differ?

1. **A couple of twenty-somethings on their first date.**

   • If dinner is the final destination for the date, this couple will want to linger and not feel rushed or as if they are "taking up a table."

   • If dinner is not the final destination for the date, but rather a chance to eat before a movie or concert, then they will have specific rate expectations. Find out what their deadlines (show times) are..

2. **Three factory-working guys, just off a double shift.**

   • This group likely will be in a hurry to get the first round of beers on the table, and their urgency will decline from there.

   • This group may be sensitive to drinks left empty for too long.

"Your most unhappy customers are your greatest source of learning."

- Bill Gates
Renegade Software Mogul

People don't go out to restaurants to eat.

Once more, think of your one-top business lady. Knowing what you do, how would you pace her meal to meet her "Rate" expectations?

- If it is happy hour, make sure to give this party plenty of notice about when specials are ending, coupled with suggestions for dinner or appetizers to share.

3. Six soccer moms together for "Girls' Night Out."

- If dinner is the main purpose and final destination for this outing, this group will want to stay a while and take it slow while they catch up. Make sure to keep drinks full and recommend plenty of add-ons (like appetizers, salads and desserts).

- If dinner is just an opportunity to meet, and is a prelude to another activity (like a show or an evening of nightclubbing), make sure to find out their schedule for the rest of the evening and adjust your service rate accordingly.

4. A young married couple and their three kids all under the age of 6.

- For parents of small children, time is of the essence. This family wants to get in and out quickly. Ask rate questions and offer to change up your steps of service. The quicker you resolve the kids' needs, the more comfortable the parents will be. Would they like to order the kids' food first while they look over the menu?

People don't go out to restaurants to eat.

Placing kids' orders early is a great trick to allow the parents to feed the kids while their own meals are being prepared.

5. Four college students in to watch "the big game."

   - For the sports fan, rate is determined by the game. You will not be turning this table until the game is over, so let the game dictate your service pace. Take advantage of commercials, time-outs and halftime to offer drinks and suggest food.

   - Be aware of the 2-minute warning (or bottom of the 9th). The end of the game can sometimes act as a natural "last call," clearing your section out all at once. Try to get fresh drinks and food items on the table at the 2-minute warning to help extend the guests' visit and get them to stay through the end-of-game exodus… and perhaps into the next game.

   You get what you focus on.

6. A visitor in from out of town, staying at the hotel down the street.

   - Guests dining alone are excruciatingly aware of time. Because there is really no conversation to distract them, they have nothing to do but count the moments it takes to get their food (or get their drinks, or pay their checks). Make sure that your

People don't go out to restaurants to eat.

rate of service is impeccable, and that you stop by the table more frequently to check in, chat, and communicate the status of the meal or drinks.

7. **Four young couples, one of which has just gotten engaged.**

   - Celebrations can be long. These guests don't want to be rushed, but can be hard to move from one dining stage to another because they are so involved in conversation with one another. The best way to pace a group like this is to make sure that there is always something coming to the table. If they are going to occupy one of your tables all night, you should at least make sure you are getting the maximum possible check total from them (lots of appetizers, soups, salads, desserts, and non-refillable beverages).

New Rule: Don't criticize a new idea unless you have a better idea!

   - When getting drink re-orders, approach each individual party guest as their beverage depletes. Trying to save yourself trips by simply asking the table at large if they are "ready for another round" will result in lower sales. No one will break conversation to take the responsibility of ordering for the entire group.

8. **Two men in business attire in for lunch.**

   - If there are papers, laptops or other electronics on

People don't go out to restaurants to eat.

the table, lunch is secondary to whatever business they are trying to accomplish. Give them plenty of time and keep interruptions to a minimum.

- If there is no work being done, but rather this is a break from work, understand that they may be on an accelerated schedule on their lunch hour, and a speedy rate of service is needed. Try time-saving steps like dropping the check when doing your food-quality check.

9. Four Senior Citizens in for breakfast

- If this is a social meal, make sure these guests do not feel rushed. Silently refill beverages without repeatedly asking if there "is anything else."

Based on what you know about your guests, try to determine the rate at which they'd like your service to go. When in doubt, ask. Delivering the expected rate of service is one of the primary factors by which your guests judge your service.

To better connect with your guests, always take the experience order first ("What brings you in today?" "What's the special occasion?" "In a hurry for lunch today, or do you have a more leisurely time frame?").

"If there is any one secret of success, it lies in the ability to get the other person's point of view and see things from that person's angle as well as from your own."

- John D. Rockefeller
Renegade Industrialist

People don't go out to restaurants to eat.

How the changing perceptions of good service may be shrinking your tips

SUMMARY

1. To be truly successful at making genuine connections with your guests, try to customize each dining or drinking experience. "Take the experience order first."

2. "**Recon**" your tables and try to observe facts about their visits that you can use to deliver a personalized dining experience.

3. Ask questions of your guests that will tell you the **regularity** of their visits. Knowing how often, if ever, they have been in your restaurant will help you decide what their needs are and what products to offer.

4. Most importantly, determine the **reason** for your guests' visits. Why they are in your restaurant will tell you almost everything you need to know about properly serving their party and exceeding their expectations.

5. Most loss of tip dollars is directly related to the timing of the guest's experience. If a guest perceives that things take too long (or even go too fast), it profoundly colors their perception of their entire visit. Find out the **rate** at which the guest expects to dine or drink, , adjust and adapt your service to suit.

Chapter 3:

Increase My Check

Preview

1. Because people primarily tip based on check total, the most fundamental technique for increasing tip income is to increase guest purchases.

2. Many common techniques associated with salesmanship have become tired and feel "fake" or "pushy" to many servers and guests.

3. Because of the pervasiveness of unemotional "up-selling" in all types of restaurant and retail interactions, consumers have developed a resistance to this dated sales method.

4. In this chapter, you will learn:

   • To treat and build your section as your own business, and make more on every sale than even the restaurant itself does.

   • How to ditch pushy sales scripts and use updated language to make genuine connections with your guests that help guide them to more & better purchases.

   • How to adjust your timing so that you are able to make just the right suggestion at just the right moment.

"When do you think you'll get a real job?"

Get a Job

Inevitably as a server or bartender, there comes a moment when someone has the raw nerve to ask you the following question:

*"When do you think you'll get a **real** job?"*

The question, aside from being rude, makes some outrageous assumptions. The greatest assumption is that waiting tables or tending bar is not a *real* job. It may not be your *permanent* job or even your *career*... but it surely is real. The hours you spend on the restaurant floor are real. The rent, mortgage, insurance and assorted other bills the job may help you pay are certainly *real* (try not paying them and find out).

Like all jobs, there are those who excel and those who simply "phone it in" and mark time. It should come as no surprise that, as with any other job, those who display focus and commitment are generally more successful and better compensated than those who do not.

The point is... whether you plan to make the service industry your career, or if it is simply a transitional

> **"It is not the employer who pays the wages. Employers only handle the money. It is the customer who pays the wages."**
>
> - Henry Ford
> *Renegade Manufacturer*

"When do you think you'll get a real job?"

gig that allows you to pay the bills while finishing school, chasing your dreams or building your future empire; *you should try to make every moment and opportunity count.* Any time spent just "going through the motions" is just that much more time placed between you and your "*real*" destination.

Speaking of time, consider how being truly engaged could give you more of *that* precious substance. If you are a full-time server working five days a week or more, think of what a *four* day work week would be like. Consider the effect that a *whole extra day every week* could have on your long-term goals, studies, mental health or social life!

By using the techniques in this chapter to increase your daily sales by 20%, you can earn as much in just four days as you currently do in five. If a 20% increase seems like a lot, consider that the average Guest spends somewhere around $15 per visit in the typical casual-theme restaurant. A 20% increase to that check is just $3... not even the price of a typical cocktail, appetizer, salad, cup of soup or dessert.

"When do you think you'll get a real job?"

Going Into Business

Take an entrepreneurial approach to restaurant work. Treat your section like your own small business. If you really think about it, it's one of the best small businesses you could own…

- It requires no advanced education, degrees or experience.

- You need no start-up money; just an interest in people and a willingness to work smart.

- Someone else (the restaurant company) has built you a beautiful storefront, paid for it, and stocked it with all the supplies and equipment you need to operate it.

- You have no rent to pay and have access to all the products you can sell at no up-front cost to you.

- Maintenance, advertising, research & development, and even taxes for your business are all paid by someone else (the Company).

- Everything you sell is generally rewarded with a generous, 15-20% cash commission (your tip), which is paid *immediately* upon closing the deal.

Most Servers earn an average of three times more on each dollar of sales than the restaurant owner does.

"When do you think you'll get a real job?"

That's far more than the Company makes! Consider that, while you make **15-20 cents** on every dollar you sell on the floor, the restaurant makes only a fraction of that.

That's right. When done correctly, *the server makes more than the restaurant company on every single dollar!*

In his perennially best-selling book, *Fundamentals: 9 Ways to be Brilliant at the New Basics of Business*, restaurant industry guru Jim Sullivan points out that most restaurants profit far less than you may think… only **5 cents** on the dollar after typical operating costs.

Payroll & Taxes 33¢

Marketing, Equipment & Insurance 20¢

Average Profit 5¢

Food & Beverage Cost 34¢

Rent & Utilities 8¢

"When do you think you'll get a real job?"

Now that you are a business owner, consider that there are four basic ways for any business to be successful:

1. Attract more customers.

2. Sell those customers as much as possible.

3. Make sure that you are charging the right price for your product, and keeping costs low ("buy low / sell high" – the most basic formula for business success).

4. Conduct your business in such a way that customers come back as soon and as often as possible, bringing their family, friends and co-workers with them (driving "frequency" or so-called "repeat business").

Think of your section or station or bar as your own store.

Market, sell and serve to maximize your profits.

Of these basic business tactics, #1 and #3 are taken care of for you by your employer.

Attracting customers (#1) is largely a function of location, marketing and advertising. The job of getting the word out about your business (your section) is already being done for you. The owner of the restaurant advertises the restaurant and devises ways to fill your section with first-time guests (a *Renegade* will then make them want to come back soon and often).

"When do you think you'll get a real job?"

The restaurant company is also taking care of the tricky tasks of inventory, purchasing, labor, pricing and cost control (#3). They have experts that are focused on competitive pricing and purchasing. It's a primary responsibility of your restaurant's Managers to track and control costs.

This leaves you with two very powerful business drivers:

- Selling your customers as much as they want to buy (#2) and

- Getting them to come back (#4).

In this chapter, we will explore by far the most powerful business tactic you can use to make more money: *selling as much as possible to the guests in your section.*

Getting your customers to come back soon and often is done by developing a regular clientele and is addressed later in Chapter 5, "Treat Me Like a Regular."

"When do you think you'll get a real job?"

Good Service = Good Tips? Not Always.

If your section is your business, then tips can be considered commissions paid on the products you sell. That commission can go up or down slightly, depending on the guest's "Tip #". 15% commission from this table, 18% from the next, etc. No matter what the percentage, all tips are based on the same thing... the check total.

Very rarely are you tipped based solely on the value of your service. The cold, hard truth is that *you primarily make money on the total that appears on the customer's bill.*

Consider iced tea. On a hot July day when you serve a tall, cool glass of iced tea to your customer, how many times will you refill it during the course of their lunch visit? 3 times? 5 times? 7? No matter how often you refill the tea glass, how many times will you be tipped on that tea *service*? Once. Period.

Always offer a non-refillable beverage first (like juice before coffee at breakfast or beer before tea at dinner), so that you are more likely to make a tip on the re-order rather than the free refill.

The same goes for coffee. Have you ever seen anyone receive their check, figure out the tip, and then add a dollar for every time you had to return to the table with a *refill*? Of course not! The plain

"When do you think you'll get a real job?"

fact is that you only get tipped once on a cup of coffee, no matter how many times you served it!! You are tipped on the coffee *purchase*, not on the coffee *service*.

If you were truly being tipped for service, wouldn't refills count?

Don't depend on "luck" to bring big checks and good tippers into your section.

Your customer's base tip is primarily determined by what appears on the bill.

That being said, isn't it in your best interest to make sure that as much as possible appears on the bill?"

Create your own luck by learning how to influence check size and tipping behaviors.

Who are the Best Tippers?

Every year, my work takes me across the country visiting restaurants, bars and nightclubs. During the course of my travels, I have the privilege of meeting and speaking before thousands of restaurant managers, servers and bartenders.

At the start of many of my workshops, I ask attendees to say who their *best, biggest* tippers are.

Although I have heard hundreds of answers to

"When do you think you'll get a real job?"

this question, (ranging from "drunken sailors" to "that creepy guy that always wears a scarf"), there are a few that always, always come up. In no particular order, they are:

1. **Regulars** - guests that come in all the time.
2. **Industry People** - restaurant / hospitality workers.
3. **Big Spenders** - guests with large checks, big parties, corporate expense accounts, or who are just trying to impress.

"Some people want it to happen, some wish it would happen, others make it happen."

- Michael Jordan
Renegade Athlete

As a service professional, you would probably agree to some extent with all of these responses – and could even add a few to the list.

These guests can be divided further into two basic types: *"Big Tippers"* and *"Big Spenders."*

Big Tippers

Your basic *Big Tipper* is someone who leaves big tips no matter what the total of their bill is.

Both *Regulars* and *Industry Workers* fall into this category, as they'll generally tip well no matter what they have purchased.

"When do you think you'll get a real job?"

They are not "straight percentage" tippers because they're trying to buy something besides good service with their tip: <u>your recognition and goodwill</u>.

The reason your recognition and goodwill are important to this group is that they plan on coming in again. They're trying to buy their way into a kind of "regular" or community status.

Big tips should not be your primary goal.

They know that regular guests get treated differently, and are willing to invest in bigger tip amounts to *get* that treatment.

Excellence should be your primary goal.

It is worth your time and effort to learn to cultivate these generous customers and attract them to your section. You will learn some great techniques for doing just that in Chapter 5, *"Treat Me Like a Regular."*

Big tips are a natural result of excellence.

Big Spenders

Big Spenders are simply guests with large checks. I frequently hear servers describe Big Spenders as guests who spend more money due the size of their party or a predisposition to drop impressive

"When do you think you'll get a real job?"

amounts of cash. Often, servers specifically identify these "whale" customers as businesspeople dining on expense accounts or members of large parties.

The average server / food-fetcher waits and hopes they get lucky and are seated with Big Spenders and their big checks as if they could *will* it to happen. *The Renegade Server* knows how to *create* Big Spenders by influencing the amount of *all* the checks in his or her section, no matter who is seated in it. No will... all skill.

More on the bill always means more in your pocket.

Throughout this book, you will find many specific ways to make unique connections with your guests so as to influence incremental increases in gratuities. Those "stand-out" behaviors are designed to encourage the guest to leave an additional dollar or two.

Consider, however, the exponential gains you will make if you use those tactics to increase the size of a tip percentage left on a much *larger total!* If you sell me two drinks instead of one, your tip doubles. No matter what "My Tip #" is. More on the bill *always* means more in your pocket.

"When do you think you'll get a real job?"

The Trouble With Salesmanship

These days, there is a lot of talk in the restaurant industry about salesmanship. Hundreds of books, workshops and training programs have been written about techniques like "Up-Selling."

In my days as a restaurant manager, I was always picking up a book or reading an article about salesmanship and bringing ideas into crew meetings to communicate to my staff.

"Salesmanship is an art. The perfection of its technique requires study and practice."

- James (JC) Penny
Renegade Retailer

The general response I received upon mentioning the word "salesmanship" was similar to what you would have seen had I begun reading a technical manual on the art of dishwasher maintenance.

Eyes instantly glossed over and my crew immediately disconnected from the meeting. Those who were at least polite enough to remain awake started doodling on their ticket books or applying make-up.

Frustrated, I decided to ask some of my best teammates why most servers had such fierce

"When do you think you'll get a real job?"

resistance to the idea of salesmanship. What was it about the techniques I was recommending that caused the disconnect?

The answers were always the same:

> *"It's pushy."*
> *"It's cheesy."*
> *"People know what they want."*

…and my personal favorite…

> *"The Company wants me to do it so they can make more sales, but there's nothing in it for me but more stuff to remember to do."*

I never considered the salesmanship tactics I was recommending to be "pushy" or "cheesy," so I wondered why my staff immediately saw them as such. If they weren't getting trained on "pushy" from me, they must be getting the idea from somewhere else.

Armed with their perceptions, I began to take a look around at what salesmanship looks like in the places my staff frequented.

If you want your life to be more rewarding, you have to change the way you think.

- Oprah Winfrey

Renegade Actress and Talk Show Host

"When do you think you'll get a real job?"

The French Fry Effect

What I saw as I began to look for salesmanship is what I would describe as the *"French Fry Effect."*

Don't just "up-sell"...

Up-*SERVE!*

Think of the last time you were in a quick-serve hamburger place. Heck, think of EVERY time you have been in a quick-serve hamburger place. Surely, each time you've ordered a hamburger in those restaurants, you were asked,

"Would you like fries with that?"

The companies that own hamburger restaurants have figured out that:

a) Some people forget to order fries with their burgers.

b) If you ask people if they want fries, they will usually buy them.

By training their counter crews to diligently ask the "French Fry Question" every time, the burger giants found out that they sold an awful lot of fries.

Soon, that type of successful "add-on" training

"When do you think you'll get a real job?"

was noticed by the greater retail community. Today, the *French Fry Effect* is used to sell everything from mega-size movie popcorn to extended warranties on electronics.

Nearly everywhere you make a purchase, the person behind the counter has been trained to offer you a larger size, a combo meal, a new variation, better brand or an accessory for the thing you originally selected. It has become known universally as an "up-sell."

Because the success of the "French Fry Question" (or "Biggie Size" question, or "Extended Warranty" question) depends on it being asked of *every single guest, every single time*, it becomes part of an automated sales process.

The average consumer is exposed to this automated sales process several times a day... every day. Nearly every purchase is now accompanied by an up-sell. It has become a "retail reflex." As a result, we as consumers have developed a reflexive resistance to the up-sell.

Besides restaurants or bars, where else have you as a customer felt you are receiving an "up-sell" pitch?

_____

_____

_____

_____

_____

_____

_____

_____

THE RENEGADE SERVER

"When do you think you'll get a real job?"

Don't think of yourself as a traditional "Salesperson."

Rather, consider yourself a "Personal Shopper" whose job it is to discern what your guests will like and present them with several options from which to choose.

Renegade Servers do not depend on automated processes. *Renegade Servers* create *unique connections* with their guests and reap the financial benefits of that relationship.

That is not to say that you shouldn't suggest items to your guests. Suggesting things that will make your guest happy is an integral part of great service! *The key is to not suggest the same thing in the same way time after time.*

Mechanical suggestions and predictable scripts benefit neither the guest nor your sales. Guests know when you are simply just pitching them something you are required to offer. Their automatic, well-rehearsed response is almost always going to be *"no."*

Guests love to buy, but hate to be "sold."

Consider the huge emotional difference between the average person's disdain for dealing with car salesmen compared to many people's *love* for shopping.

"When do you think you'll get a real job?"

Both events end in a purchase, so why the big difference? *The answer is approach.* The car salesman is perceived as pushy because he will do or say anything to get you to buy the product *he* wants you to buy. Shopping is considered fun because you are presented with many options from which to choose the thing that will make *you* happy.

Mechanical sales pitches can make guests feel like the salesperson is just trying to tack on more things they don't need or want just to make a sale. Just like what happened to them on the car lot or at the 'big box' electronics store.

Do unto others as they would have you do unto them.

Truly successful salesmanship comes from first connecting with the guest by engaging in real conversations that discover their needs, desires and tastes; then pairing them up with just the right product.

To that end, there are 2 major factors that can affect your success in increasing *both* your guest's bill *and* their *satisfaction*:

Language (what you say) &
Timing (when you say it)

"When do you think you'll get a real job?"

Language

Have you ever had someone ask you, "Hey, what's happening?"... and you answered "Fine." Or conversely... "How's it going?" to which you mistakenly answered "Not much."

Basically, these two greetings are used so much that they have become inter-changeable. We are so accustomed to hearing these questions, that our brains have the answer formulated before they are even asked... and it really doesn't *matter* which one is asked.

The words have stopped having value for us. They are very different questions... but we now accept them to have the same meaning, which is "hello."

Countless times, I have been at the snack counter at the movies and caught myself letting this kind of language slip occur. After buying my popcorn and candy, the cashier almost always says "thanks, and enjoy your show." To which I almost always reply "*You too!*"

Can you think of any other everyday phrases that are used so often, they have lost their meanings?

"When do you think you'll get a real job?"

"You, too?" The *cashier* isn't going to see a movie! I am just replying to his "have a nice day" tone.

Restaurant-Speak

The same thing happens in restaurants today. A certain language has developed. I call it *restaurant-speak*. It is just so much "verbal wallpaper" that just prompts the guest to tell the server what to go and get for them. It is the main reason that restaurant dining has become a process versus a pleasure.

If you don't like the idea of using a "pushy" sales script, consider that, by using "restaurant speak" you are already scripted... by default.

Rather than a genuine exchange between two people, we have developed this restaurant-speak system of "call-and-response" that moves the dining experience along and reduces the server to a "food fetcher."

Using restaurant-speak will never make you more tips.

It will not help you stand out against the background of your restaurant and make a real, personal connection with your guest. If you act and sound the same as every other server, you are essentially interchangeable with every other server.

"When do you think you'll get a real job?"

Restaurant-speak places *process* before *people* (how many are you, what do you want, what can I get you… etc.).

These questions are designed to communicate just the information needed to complete the "process" of dining. By using this language, you essentially become a cog in the restaurant machine.

If you doubt that dining out these days has become a process, try this exercise. The next time you and your friends go out to eat, play the game of "Restaurant-Speak."

To play, all you have to do is try to guess which standard phrase or question your server will use on his next visit to your table. These phrases have become so common, that even your friends and family who are not "in the business" will be able to play. Here is how it will likely go:

"I try to always think of and refer to my guests as 'people' or 'parties'… never just 'tables'."

- Sean Pointer
Renegade Server

Host: *"Hi, two?"*

"Just one?"

"Right this way."

"Our specials are listed here."

"Roger will be your server."

"When do you think you'll get a real job?"

Bartender: *"Hey Guys."*

"What can I getcha?"

"Ready for another?"

Server: *"Hi. My name's Roger. I'll be your server today."*

"Can I start you guys off with something to drink?"

"Have you had a chance to look at the menu?"

"Do you need a few minutes?"

"How is everything? O.K.?"

"Are you still working on that?"

"Did anyone save room for dessert?"

"I can take this whenever you're ready."

"Did you need any change on this?"

"Thanks! Come back and see us."

What are some more examples of "Restaurant Speak" that you are practically guaranteed to hear from a server?

_____

_____

_____

_____

_____

_____

_____

_____

All of these phrases get the job done.
They will likely get you to the guest's "Tip #."

But if you want the guest to rise above his "Tip #," you're gong to have to make some kind of impression on him, and those phrases aren't going to do the trick.

THE RENEGADE SERVER

"When do you think you'll get a real job?"

Scan this code to see how language can set you apart!

If you use any of the above restaurant-speak phrases, you are definitely doing it the way nearly every other server is.

To become a *Renegade Server,* remove them from your vocabulary *today* and begin enjoying exponentially bigger tips.

By simply not using the same words as every other server in America, you will begin setting yourself apart and making lasting impressions on your guests.

A Food-Fetcher Asks

How Many?

What can I get you?

Have you decided on anything?

Do you want fries with that?

How is everything, OK?

A *Renegade* Asks

How are you?

What brings you in today?

Have you ever been here before?

Do you like chocolate?

How did we do on your steak? Is it just the way you like it?

"When do you think you'll get a real job?"

Here are some alternatives that put the "people" back on top:

"Hi. My name's Roger. I'll be your server today."

No kidding. That explains why you're standing next to my table with a pad and tray.

Try *"How are you?"*, *"What brings you in to-day?"* or *"Have you ever dined with us before?"*

All of these are proper, personal greetings and can help you get more information about the guests' expectations.

"Can I start you guys off with something to drink?"

There are thousands of drink possibilities in the average restaurant. Every restaurant has tap water and iced tea. Neither of which are very healthy choices for your tip.

Your first beverage approach is your only opportunity to get guests into a beverage that will help you improve your tip line.

Don't waste it!

"When do you think you'll get a real job?"

Think of some more, different ways to say "Can I get you something to drink?"

The first beverage approach is your *only* opportunity to help guide guests into a beverage purchase that will give them a better experience and help you improve the tip line! Once they order that glass of tap water, there's no going back!! Suggest something! Anything!

Try *"Since this is your first time here, may I suggest you try one of our world-famous hand-scooped milkshakes?"*

"Have you had a chance to look at the menu?"

The menus are on the table. What you really want to know is what *else* you can put on the table for them. If they haven't decided, make some suggestions, or offer to bring them a shareable appetizer while they take their time and make up their minds.

Try *"If you haven't gotten to it yet, check out the Grilled Chipotle Chicken Salad. It's the staff favorite."*

"When do you think you'll get a real job?"

"How is everything? O.K.?"

There are two problems with this question. The first is asking about "everything." When we ask about "everything," "anything," everyone," or "anyone," we really mean *nothing*, and speak to *no one*.

Be specific! In order to make a *real* personal connection, ask if their steaks are cooked just the way they like them or if they are happy with your salmon recommendation.

"It's the little details that are vital. Little things make big things happen."

- John Wooden
Renegade Coach

The second problem is asking if everything is O.K. If "O.K." is your goal, you really should aim a little higher.

Try *"Isn't the Mahi Mahi delicious?"*

"Are you still working on that?"

If there is still food on the plate, leave it until the guest makes it clear that they are finished. If the

"When do you think you'll get a real job?"

plate is empty, remove it. It's that simple. If you are really not sure, ask if they would like you to clear the plate. Eating in your restaurant should never be referred to as *"work."* Guests should *enjoy* your food, not have to *work* at it.

 "Did anyone save room for dessert?"

Has anyone *ever* said yes to this question?!? This is another phrase that has become so commonplace that it has lost its real meaning. Today, this question only prompts the answer *"no."* It assumes that if one hasn't *"saved"* room, it's too late to do anything about it now.

For more great ideas on how to sell more desserts, see the Quick Tips section at the back of this book.

I can't think of a *worse* time to begin a dessert conversation than right after the guest has stuffed themselves with dinner (a fact reinforced by the *question itself!*). The dessert conversation should begin long before dinner is over.

 Ask a guest if she likes chocolate, for example. A *"yes"* answer will allow you to start a natural

"When do you think you'll get a real job?"

conversation about your dessert options that have chocolate in them. A *"no"* answer will lead to a conversation about those items that don't have chocolate, like cheesecake or apple pie.

Ask if your guests would like to order a slice of pie or a Coke float to enjoy while their meal *"settles."* Many times a guest will tell you they are too full, and *"couldn't possibly"* add a dessert. If a guest is in *"food coma"* after a big meal, remind them that sugar (dessert) or caffeine (coffee drinks) might be just what the Doctor ordered to perk them back up.

Instead of saying "would you like to start with an appetizer?" say this instead:

"Have you ever tried our famous beer battered onion rings or Chicken Diablo Nachos?"

It's soft-selling, and it works.

You should also remind them that all of your delicious desserts come with two (or three) forks for sharing and are available to take home (or back to the office, or babysitter) and enjoy when they're hungry again.

"I can take this whenever you're ready."

"When do you think you'll get a real job?"

The Check Drop

Suggestive Selling is helping the guest make a decision that's just right for them.

The Check Drop is one of your last opportunities to make an impression on your guests before they decide what size tip they are going to leave. The *last* thing you want to do is leave them with a *"whenever"*-based statement. Use this opportunity to reinforce the awesome quality of your service.

Try saying, *"before I give you your bill, let me make sure everything is just right. Did you enjoy yourself today?"* This will give you one last chance to right any wrongs before the guest decides on your tip. If everything went great, you are actually having the guest <u>say so</u>. What a great last thought to leave in her mind when signing that check!

"Did you need any change on this?"

This question is rude because it assumes a tip. It is a prime example of putting process before

"When do you think you'll get a real job?"

people. It basically says *"If it's all the same to you, I'd rather not make another trip back to this table if I don't have to."* Always remember to portray the image that tips are accepted, but never expected. Returning with change gives you another chance to interact with your guest and possibly increase that tip.

To make genuine connections with your guests, always ask questions about **_them_**, not questions that simply serve the process.

"Thank you for your business! My name's Stacey. Please ask for me next time you come in. I'll still be checking on you, in case you change your mind about that Vanilla Bean Cheesecake."

"Thanks, you guys! Come back and see us."

There is nothing terribly wrong with this statement. It is polite. It's just that overuse has robbed it of any genuine meaning and turned it into so much *"verbal wallpaper."*

Every guest should receive thanks and an invitation to return. Just do it with words that matter.

"When do you think you'll get a real job?"

"Thank you for your business. I hope you enjoyed yourself. I wrote my name on your copy of your receipt, so you can make sure to ask for me next time you come in!"

Timing

Timing is one reason that many of the standard sales techniques used in restaurants come off as sounding *"pushy."*

<u>When</u> you suggest something makes a huge difference regarding the success of your suggestion!

Timing is the key to merchandising the menu.

Think of the last time someone asked you an up-selling *"French Fry Question."* Chances are it was <u>after</u> you had already decided what you wanted and ordered.

Guest: *"I'll have a margarita."*
Server: *"Would you like that made with Cuervo?"*

The *"French Fry Question"* is asked in an effort to get you to buy something different, larger or more expensive. Almost every up-selling technique is designed to change or build-upon something the

"When do you think you'll get a real job?"

customer has already ordered. Waiting for someone to decide, then changing their mind is hard!

Wouldn't it have been much easier to get in earlier on the guest's decision-making process, and help *guide* them into a decision rather than try to change their mind?

Here are 6 suggestions for using correct timing to make your suggestions more successful:

Get In Early

An undecided guest is the greatest sales opportunity in any restaurant or bar! Rather than waiting for the guest to make a decision and then trying to change that decision, try adjusting your timing to get in on the decision-making process. Don't wait until a guest has already ordered to make a suggestion, catch them while they are undecided!

The greatest sales opportunity in any restaurant is an undecided guest.

A great example of how servers use early timing is when communicating specials. Specials are generally communicated to the diner before their decision-making process has begun. Imagine how

"When do you think you'll get a real job?"

much tougher it would be to sell today's lunch special if you waited until the guest had decided before you mentioned it. You would fail! And yet, many servers do the same thing when trying to up-sell other items.

If you wait for your guest to order a cocktail, and then try to move them into a premium label, you are trying to *"correct"* their order, not genuinely guide them into a better purchase.

For more ideas on how to sell more appetizers and add-ons, check out the Quick Tips section at the back of thisbook.

Rather than waiting for the guest to initiate the order, then trying to change it, get in early with a suggestion:

Server: *"Since this is your first time here, I recommend you try our famous 'Mango-Rita'. It has been our most popular cocktail for 15 years."*

Now, the guest may still choose to order a regular margarita… but it would be much tougher to do so after finding out about the signature item!

Again: people love to buy, but hate to be *"sold."* When trying to move them from the drink they have ordered into a slightly more expensive

"When do you think you'll get a real job?"

version, a guest may feel a bit of sales pressure. By describing the premium item right out of the gate, the guest is simply being given options, from which they can "shop."

The real point here is to mention the things you want to sell <u>before</u> the guest has made another decision. If you want to sell your special appetizer, mention it before drinks have been ordered. If you want to sell a specialty beverage, make it part of your first approach. If you want to sell desserts, mention them during your food check-back:

Connect with every guest before you try to "sell" them.

Timing *Suggest*

First Approach	Juice or Coffee at Breakfast, Specialty Drinks, Appetizers
Beverage Delivery	Food Specials
Appetizer Delivery	Wine
Food Delivery	Dessert, Drink Re-Orders
Food Check-Back	After Dinner Drink

"When do you think you'll get a real job?"

Table Trends

Sometimes servers actually let the natural timing of the ordering process rob them of sales. Many servers begin taking an order at one corner of the table and then work around the table in a clockwise (or counterclockwise) fashion until all of the orders have been taken. The process is easy to remember, can help you keep track of which guest gets what, and it helps maintain order. *It also can cost you precious dollars on the check.*

When approaching a guest, always be prepared to recommend something. Be able to describe one thing you like, and one thing that is very popular with other guests.

Have you ever approached a table, started taking drink orders and had Guest #1 order an iced tea? Often, what happens is that Guest #2 will then also order tea, and so will Guest #3, and so it cascades around the table.

Orders of beverages and other additional items (like salads and desserts) are often dictated by these "table trends." Whatever is ordered first is likely to be ordered by all.

Chances are if Guest #1 had ordered a beer or cocktail, it would have unlocked premium beverage purchases all around the table.

"When do you think you'll get a real job?"

Clearly, a key to selling more premium drinks (or appetizers, sides or salads) is to *start* with the guest who will *order* one. If you always start taking orders based solely on seating position, you are assigning the most important purchase to pure, random chance.

Find the Buyer

Instead of letting random seating position dictate who places those all-important first orders, you should seek out the person who wants to make the purchase <u>you</u> want and start the desired table-trend.

Always maintain eye contact when the Guest is speaking.

Don't start based on position. Start by finding the person who *wants* an appetizer, salad, soup or premium drink. Approach your table and ask who is buying what you are selling. If you can get the Buyer to identify himself, the likelihood of the rest of the table following the trend is much higher. Ask for the Buyer to identify him- or herself, and work around from there:

"<u>Who</u> will have a salad with lunch?

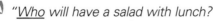

"When do you think you'll get a real job?"

Instead of starting around the table with:

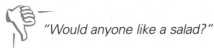

"Would anyone like a salad?"

This small change in approach will often identify the person interested in buying, and yield the correct purchase. From there you can work in any order you like. Taking orders according to seating order has the chance of yielding a bad (low-tip-making) response that will likely be echoed by everyone around the table.**

Even when you are really busy, always take a moment to stop by a Guest's table (or bar seat) that has just been seated and smile and say "*I'll be right with you!*"

**NOTE – No matter how you take the order, the guests should still be served ladies first. You can still take the orders out of sequence, but write it down in the order in which they are sitting.

Guest-Driven Timing

The quickest way to stop being a "food-fetcher," and become a *Renegade Server* is to let the guest dictate the timing of your sales.

Rather than prompting the guest to buy at predictable intervals (*can I get you something to drink... did anyone save room for dessert...*), watch for signs that the guest wants or needs help deciding.

"When do you think you'll get a real job?"

**Guests give us windows
all the time during which it is easy
to step in and make a sale!**

I used to be a bartender in a very high-volume nightclub. Countless times on a busy Friday or Saturday night, I would come across a common, frustrating situation.

My bar would be slammed, and I was working at top speed. Although I tried to acknowledge every guest as soon as they approached my bar, the wait for a drink was often several minutes.

Frequently, after a long wait, I would approach a guest, apologize for the wait and thank him for his patience… only to find out that he _still_ didn't know what he wanted to drink!!!

Hadn't I given him enough time?!? Wasn't he thinking about it while he was waiting?!?

Naturally, my next act was to leave him hanging for a while longer while he made up his mind and I tended to other guests. My desertion was done

Allowing guests to struggle with a menu decision by "giving them" a few more minutes increases both the number of trips you must make to the table and the time it takes you to turn it *(effectively reducing the number of guests you can serve).*

"When do you think you'll get a real job?"

half so that I could get on with helping the other customers and half to punish *"Mr. Indecisive"* for wasting my time and not having his act together.

When you "give" guests a few minutes, you really take those minutes away from yourself!

This scenario plays out not only at busy bars, but at countless dinner tables every day. How often have you approached a table to take an order, only to find out that no one knows what they want?

If your reaction to a table of undecided guests is to cheerfully say *"I'll give you a few minutes"* and walk away, I urge you to reconsider. *You are losing money.*

I learned the hard way during my bartending days that not only was my "desertion" tactic frustrating my guest (and making my tips go way down), it was also causing me to double or triple the amount of time it took me to get that first drink order – thereby robbing me of valuable time I could be spending taking more orders *and making more tips.*

Now I realize that guests who haven't decided are really just giving me an opportunity to sell them what I want them to have!

"When do you think you'll get a real job?"

Rather than give them "more time" to make a decision (which means delaying their order, and reducing the total number of guests I can help that day), I should be helping them make a decision *NOW*, using that opportunity to suggest signature items that will have the greatest impact on the guest's satisfaction, the check and my TIP.

Instead of seeing a guest's indecision as an inconvenience or an opportunity to escape the table and delay service, see it for what it is – a natural chance to serve better and sell more.

Scan this code to see how timing and indecision can help you sell more!

If a guest at breakfast hasn't made up his mind, offer to bring a muffin or scone *while he decides*. At lunch or dinner, offer appetizers to share while they relax and peruse the menu.

If a guest still doesn't know what he'd like to order after an appropriate amount of time with the menu, always have something ready to suggest.

I recommend always being prepared with one item you really like, and one item that is very popular with other guests.

"When do you think you'll get a real job?"

Better still, guide the guest by asking appropriate questions like *"Well, let's start with the basics: are you a little hungry or a lot hungry?"* Now, lead them through the decision making process.

If guests still want more time to decide, it is a great time to recommend starters like soups and salads to eat *while* they make their decision.

Guests can be strongly influenced by what's going on in the restaurant around them. You may notice that the very act of selling and serving more items like cocktails, appetizers and desserts will cause more guests to buy them.

Make sure they are visible!

Merchandise Your Products

The easiest way for any business to sell a product is to display it in a positive way to potential customers. Department stores have display windows and mannequins, auto dealers have showrooms, and you have your menu and your section.

Have you ever heard someone say that something is so good it practically "sells itself?" In the restaurant business, that usually refers to an item that looks so big, unusual or delicious that people want to buy it after just *seeing* it.

I once worked in a restaurant that featured a HUGE piece of chocolate cake called "Chocolate Danger."

"When do you think you'll get a real job?"

The cake had 5 layers, and was at least 10 inches tall. The frosting between the layers alternated between a dark chocolate ganache, cream-cheese frosting and a whipped hazelnut crème. It was topped with semisweet chocolate curls and served with a scoop of French vanilla ice cream. It was the most decadent looking dessert I have ever seen.

Without fail, as soon as one of these monsters was out on a table, other guests asked about it. In fact, I started noticing that once a piece of Chocolate Danger had been sold; there was a chain reaction throughout the dining room creating more sales.

Having noticed that, I started adjusting my delivery routes through the dining room when carrying a slice of Chocolate Danger. I purposefully, slowly walked by every one of my tables.

If I had to do a check-back, I did so with Chocolate Danger on my tray. If someone needed to re-order a beverage, I took the

Multiply the number of $5 desserts you think you can sell per day by 250 to find out how much more it could mean to you in annual tip income (assume a 5-day work week and 20% tips).

"When do you think you'll get a real job?"

order on my way to the Chocolate Danger table. If someone needed to be greeted, I did so with Chocolate Danger in my hand. Chocolate Danger was my #1 product, and I used every opportunity I could to display it to my section. I rarely actually talked about it, but it was usually at my side.

What are some things on your menu that look so good they "sell themselves?"

Before long, I was selling Chocolate Danger to over half of my tables – up to 15 a day.

At about $9 apiece, that was $135 per day in Chocolate danger sales. My usual 20% tip on that was an additional $27 per day. That's an extra $540 in an average month (coincidentally, pretty close to my rent at the time)! Chocolate Danger paid my rent!!

If you want to move your customers to buy signature items, let them see them throughout their visit. There is no need to wait until the end of the meal to show off desserts.

Do you have an entrée platter on the menu that sizzles, smokes or just looks extra-delicious? Waffles piled with fruit and whipped cream? An appetizer sampler platter that is stacked up to the

"When do you think you'll get a real job?"

sky? A particularly decadent looking dessert? What about a colorfully garnished margarita or giant beer?

Whatever it is; if it has a particularly appealing look, display it on your way through your section and watch your sales skyrocket without ever having to say a word.

Time Checks

Did you (or someone you know) ever have a real piece-of-junk car? You know; the kind of ride that makes you pray that you hit all green lights... because if you get stopped at a red, the thing may never get started again?

Think of the guest experience in a restaurant (and especially a bar) as that old, heap of a car. The only thing keeping it moving forward is inertia. Once it stops, it may not get started again. It is your job to keep it moving forward.

Keeping the guest engaged *and buying* is definitely to your advantage. If you can keep the guest engaged long enough to turn one beer into two beers (or one juice into two), you have essentially *doubled* your tip.

"Opportunities are like buses... there's always another one coming."

- Richard Branson
Renegade Billionaire

"When do you think you'll get a real job?"

There are several moments during which guests pause and consider whether they should stay and have one more drink (or dessert, or coffee...) or if it is time for them to go. These small moments of truth I call "Time Checks."

Scan this code to see video on how to turn one drink into two!

A Time Check is represented by that moment when the guest disengages, looks at his watch and asks for the check. The most dangerous time to allow one of these events is towards the end of the entrée, but before dessert or beverage re-order.

We've all seen it a million times: the question is... how do we prevent it? One of the best techniques is timing.

Permission Purchasing... how to turn "Just One Beer" into "Guys' Night Out"

Let's say you and I just got off from a hard day's work together, and decide to go out for "just one beer" (ahh... the infamous "just one beer"). We sit down, order, and the server brings us two tall frosty beers.

"When do you think you'll get a real job?"

Now, you are more thirsty than I am (plus, I'm not a very fast drinker), so by the time you are finished with your first beer, I am little more than halfway.

The server appears and asks you if you'd like another beer.

What do you do?

If you are like the vast majority of people, you will **look at my beer**, in order to decide if you will have another. You will probably reason (in your mind) that if you drank a whole beer in the time it took me to finish the *first* half of mine; *surely*, you can drink a second in the time it takes me to finish.

This same reflex often happens when dessert is offered. If you notice a guest looking at their companion when you ask if they want dessert, they **do**… they are just trying to gauge whether the other person does, too. This is the perfect time to suggest a *shared* dessert.

The server quickly brings you your *second* beer (ahh… the infamous "just one beer"). Sure enough,

"We are not in the coffee business serving people, we are in the people business serving coffee"

- Howard Schultz
Renegade CEO, Starbucks

"When do you think you'll get a real job?"

just as I am finishing up, you are about halfway into number two.

When you and a friend are drinking, and the bartender asks if you'd like another... do you look down at your own glass first, or at your friend's in order to decide?

Our clever server notices that I am empty and asks if I'd like another. I decide *by looking to see how much beer you have left.*

You see where I'm going. One thing leads to another, and suddenly "just one beer" has turned into a fun night of partying, an impromptu scavenger hunt, and the makings of a wicked hangover.

By a simple trick of timing, our server has turned a sale of one beer apiece into a fat bar tab and an even fatter tip.

Consider for a moment, however, how things might have gone had she waited for both of our glasses to empty, and tried to recommend another "round" in the beginning.

"When do you think you'll get a real job?"

The sight of two empty glasses gives neither of us anything to use in reasoning ourselves into another beer! The only way for us to gauge the timing of our round is to look at our watches. Looking at watches is *bad news* in our business… ever see a clock on the wall in a bar, nightclub or casino?

That Time Check lets us know that we have succeeded in having just one beer.

Anytime a server asks if guests would like "another round," and a guest looks at his watch, it is usually followed by the phrase:

"Naahh… go ahead and close us out."

The server has essentially provided a time-based exit event. The guest will close out the check and stop spending (tipping).

For ideas on how to use *refillable* beverages to increase your tips, check out the Quick Tips section at the back of this book.

To avoid this Time Check, remember two things:

1. **Sell to the Empty** – Get to the empty glass as soon as you can, and preferably while the companion's drink is as full as possible. It will provide time-based reasoning based on the *full drink* – not actual time. It is important to get there when only one glass is empty… two empty

"When do you think you'll get a real job?"

"My formula is pretty simple. The more positive energy you give your customers, the longer they stay. The longer they stay, the more they spend. The more they spend, the more you and your bar make. A happy customer becomes an advertising agent for your bar, and you can't pay for word of mouth. You have to earn it every day."

- Joe Frisch
Renegade Bartender,
Georgia

glasses may lead to closing out the check (a Time Check). If you do get to the table late and see two nearly empty glasses, offer to bring two new beverages by <u>name</u> ("*Another Bacardi and Diet Coke and Autumn Wheat Beer?*").

2. **Sell Drinks, Not "Rounds"** – Always offer individual drinks. No one likes to be responsible for ordering for everyone. Additionally, a "round" sounds like a time commitment. Notice how many people around a table look at their watch anytime you recommend another round. Instead, approach individuals, and offer to refill their specific beverages.

Being on the Guest's Side

If the subject of salesmanship still feels uncomfortable to you because you feel as if you are just "pushing product" on the guest in order to serve the Company, I urge you to rethink.

You do not have to be *against* the guest to be *for* the restaurant. It is only by using "restaurant-speak" sales pitches and mechanical timing that a server comes across as a mercenary cog in the restaurant machine.

"When do you think you'll get a real job?"

The best interests of the restaurant, the guest and the server are not mutually exclusive.

The important thing to remember relative to the art of increasing checks is that, when done correctly, it is a win-win-win situation.

The Restaurant wins.
Higher sales mean healthier businesses. A healthier, busier restaurant can provide you with more shifts, more tables and, ultimately more earning opportunities.

You win.
Since the vast majority of gratuities are based on the check total, boosting that total is clearly the best way to increase your own income.

You're only as good as your last happy customer.

The Guest wins.
In general, the guest who has been exposed to everything your restaurant has to offer has the best experience. Being informed about specials or signature items serves to make the guest experience richer and more unique. In fact, research shows that guests who buy more not only tip a higher percentage, but they score the quality of their experience higher, too!

"When do you think you'll get a real job?"

GUEST CHECK

2 Iced Tea	1.99
	1.99
2 Diet Cola	1.99
	1.99
Chix Caes	10.49
Burg/Fries	8.99
Ribs	13.49
Chix Pasta	12.29
tax	3.87
	57.09

Your 15% Tip $8.56

New Tip $13.20

GUEST CHECK

Finding the Buyer, rather than leaving to chance

Mango-Rita	6.79
2 Diet Coke	3.99
	3.99
2 Dos Equis	1.99
	1.99
Chix Caesar	10.49
Killer Nachos	7.49
BBQ Ribs	13.49
Side Salad	1.60
Burg/Fries	8.49
Chix Pasta	12.29
Choc Danger!!	8.99
tax	5.91
	$88.00

Non-refillable beverages increase your tip each time they go to the table!

Use Guest-driven timing to suggest share-able appetizers

Ask about soup or salad every time!

Show off your crave-able desserts!

"When do you think you'll get a real job?"

SUMMARY

1. Your guest's base tip is primarily determined by what appears on the bill.

2. You will have greater success selling to your guests if you establish a genuine connection by avoiding "restaurant-speak."

3. Try to anticipate your guests' desires and recommend items early. Suggestive Selling is much easier than waiting for them to order, and then trying to change their minds (up-selling).

4. Try to locate and <u>begin</u> <u>with</u> the guest who is likely to buy what you want to sell. Don't leave it to chance or seating order.

5. Show off great looking add-on items by walking them through your section.

6. Sell additional drinks by taking drink orders before multiple glasses go empty.

7. Suggesting special products enriches the Guest Experience.

Chapter 4:
Stand Out

Preview

1. Because many guests have come to view the modern casual dining experience as "process," it is very easy for them to view you as **part** of that process.

2. In order to make more tips, it is essential that you are seen by your guest as a real **person** rather than simply a "cog" in the restaurant machine.

3. The key to connecting with your guests and being seen as a real person is to add a couple of items or behaviors that make you distinct from other servers. Be one **in** a million, not one **of** a million.

4. In this chapter, you will learn:

   - How to make yourself physically distinct, while still conforming with your restaurant's uniform dress code.

   - How to provide brief, genuine moments of connection with your guests during which they recognize you on a personal level.

The key to being a Renegade and making more money is being seen as a person, not a food-fetcher.

The key to being a Renegade and making more money is being seen as a person, not a food-fetcher.

There is a restaurant in my neighborhood that's always busy and is large enough to employ about 40 or 50 servers. I'm not really a regular there, though my wife and I stop in for dinner once every couple of months or so. Because of the immense size of the place and the army of servers that work the dining room, I can't ever recall getting the same server twice. I do, however, remember getting a particular server *once*.

All of the servers at this restaurant are required to wear what I would consider a pretty standard "Casual Dining" uniform. Black pants. Black, short-sleeved, collared shirt with logo. Black server apron. Nametag.

During one visit, my wife and I had been seated and had just picked up our menus. A young waitress approached our table with an enormous, engaging smile and asked if "anyone needed a margarita as much as *she* did." It was a hot

> "To give real service you must add something which cannot be bought or measured with money, and that is sincerity and integrity."
>
> - Douglas Adams
> *Renegade Novelist*

The key to being a Renegade and making more money is being seen as a person, not a food-fetcher.

Saturday afternoon and I had planned on maybe having a cold beer, but there's just something about hearing the word *"margarita"* that makes you want one. Plus, I kind of felt like I would be doing this smiling server a favor, and that maybe – just maybe – she would enjoy that margarita vicariously through me.

Sign on Tip Jar:

"If you fear change, leave it here!"

My wife and I both took her up on her offer of margaritas and, as she took out her server book to write down our order, I noticed that she had stuck a bumper sticker to the back of her ticket book that read "I ♥ DORKS."

Ever the clever comedienne, my wife – who " ♥'s" *me* – told her *"I see we have something in common!"* Meaning, of course, my wife thinks I'm a dork… hilarious.

As I rolled my eyes, the server put her hand on my wife's shoulder and replied, *"Yes, ma'am, we clearly both like <u>margaritas</u>."* We all laughed, and I felt like we had become fast friends.

The rest of her service was just as outstanding, as well. Naturally, that server was treated very

The key to being a Renegade and making more money is being seen as a person, not a food-fetcher.

well by us in the tip department (after all, we had become *friends*!).

That dining experience has stood out in my mind ever since. Although I can't recall the meal itself, what I do recall is how the personality of our server stood out and how we all had a good laugh together. We have been back to that restaurant many times since that afternoon, and are always on the lookout for our friend who " ♥'s DORKS."

Scan this code for an idea of how to be seen as an individual to your Guests!

What Went Right:

Obviously, our server's first brilliant move was getting us to order two signature margaritas. At $7.49 apiece, I'm sure our server was much happier with my 20% base tip on our $15.00 worth of margaritas as opposed to the $7.50 we would have spent on two beers priced at $3.75 each. Just by suggesting a premium beverage choice, she *doubled* her gratuity on our drinks!

Naturally, upon receiving our check, I figured out my usual 20%, and actually threw in an extra

The key to being a Renegade and making more money is being seen as a person, not a food-fetcher.

$4.00 on top. The reason? We felt like we had made a personal connection with our server and wanted to treat her like a friend.

"It's O.K. to be crazy, but don't be insane."

- Sean "Diddy" Combs
Renegade Music Mogul

How did she open up that connection and, more importantly, how can you learn to do the same? Find subtle, genuine ways to communicate your humanity and individuality to the guest."

Use Your Teeth

After all this time, I can still remember the big, tooth-filled smile with which our server approached the table. It may sound simple, but smiling really has a profound effect on tips. I know it is a basic tenet of the customer service business, but you would be surprised at how many servers, bartenders and other salespeople forget this important ingredient!

I'm not just talking about a polite grin as you say hello. The type of smile that makes a *real* difference is the big, wide, open-mouth, "*It's-my-birthday, thank-you-for-the-puppy*" kind of smile. The kind of smile that uses your whole face and almost makes you close your eyes. Practice; it's worth it.

The key to being a Renegade and making more money is being seen as a person, not a food-fetcher.

In a study conducted by Dutch social scientists, the power of the BIG smile was very apparent. Several servers waiting on guests in a cocktail lounge were randomly assigned the condition of either greeting their guests with a large, open-mouthed smile or a small closed-lipped smile.

At the conclusion of the study, the guests who received the little grins left an average of 20 cents, while the recipients of the big smiles tipped 48 cents (remember... they're Dutch).

That is a 140% increase in tips for smiling bigger!!!

Be Distinct

In today's casual dining culture, it is too easy to blend in to the restaurant and become part of the "process" of chain dining. If you are simply an average "food fetcher," you will make *average* money.

If you are able to present yourself as a distinct, individual human being with a life and a story,

"The more you like yourself, the less you are like everyone else, which makes you unique."

- Walt Disney
Renegade Animator

The key to being a Renegade and making more money is being seen as a person, not a food-fetcher.

you will be able to make a personal connection on some level with your guests. If you are able to connect on a personal level, your guests will actually *care* about what you think of their tip!!

In the restaurant business, the word *uniform* should be a noun, not an adjective.

Notice that one of the first things that drew my wife and me to connect with the server in the story was the funny bumper sticker on the back of her check-book.

Of course your attire should comply to your company's policies.

In a sea of black shirts, she made herself *physically distinct*. While I am a big believer in appearing for work in a clean, crisp, regulation uniform; I also recommend displaying some personal style and unique personality... but remember to first be interested, then be interesting.

Your personality and service style should *never* be able to be described as *uniform*!

A study in the *Journal of Applied Communication Research* titled "She Wore a Flower in Her Hair: The Effect of Ornamentation on Non-verbal Communication," highlights the gratuity benefits of making yourself physically distinct.

In the study, six female servers agreed to track

The key to being a Renegade and making more money is being seen as a person, not a food-fetcher.

their tips over four shifts. For two of the shifts, each of the servers agreed to wear a flower in her hair.

The results indicated that the servers made an average of $1.50 per guest in tips when not wearing the flower, as opposed to $1.75 per guest when they were adorned with a bloom.

That is a 17% increase in tips just by wearing a flower!!!

Have a unique way you stand out and connect with guests? Share it on our Facebook page (Renegade Hospitality) and give us a "Like" while you're there!

Clearly, the results of this study indicate that wearing something unique can have the effect of personalizing you to your guest, and result in a dramatic increase in tips.

Besides a flower or bumper sticker, I have seen effective use of:

- Interesting and unusual neckties
- Creative nametags
- Colorful scarves
- Unique jewelry or hats
- Stickers or photos on your check-minder

THE RENEGADE SERVER

The key to being a Renegade and making more money is being seen as a person, not a food-fetcher.

A final word of caution: *Don't Get Too Cute*.

1. Stay within the boundaries of what is acceptable (and allowed) for your restaurant. It may not be appropriate to wear a hat or scarf in a fine dining establishment. Likewise, some restaurants pride themselves in the uniform appearance of their staff; right down to matching pens and pencils. Never fear… there are other ways to endear yourself to your guest on a personal level without fighting company policy.

Remember this server from the movie Office Space?

2. Don't get carried away. One of the hallmarks of the cheesy corporate server is the suspender or vest littered with message buttons. I strongly caution anyone against covering one's self in corny phrases, as it can appear fake and, ultimately, have the opposite, undesirable effect of making you look like a corporate cog (ever seen the movie *Office Space*?).

3. It should go without saying that messages that take a political, controversial or religious stand are not appropriate for the workplace. Remember, you are trying to ingratiate yourself to the maximum possible number of people. Controversial messages (by their very nature) can only serve to alienate some people from you.

The key to being a Renegade and making more money is being seen as a person, not a food-fetcher.

Touchy, Touchy

You may recall that, during her interaction at our table, our server placed her hand briefly on my wife's shoulder while addressing her. Believe it or not, this may be one of the least known, seldom used yet *most effective* ways to connect with your guests.

Learn other ways to subtly influence guest behavior in the "Quick Tips"section in the back of this book.

Making brief physical contact with others is an ancient way to convey safety, friendliness and goodwill. It is quite natural and, if done correctly, can be the most appropriate, professional thing in the world. Consider the handshake; is there anything more businesslike and acceptable in public situations?

The effect of casual touching (noticed and subliminal) has been often researched. In fact, many scientific papers have been written specifically about the effect of casual contact in the restaurant environment.

Research shows that a brief, casual touch on the shoulder of a seated guest (while clearing

The key to being a Renegade and making more money is being seen as a person, not a food-fetcher.

plates or dropping the check) or on the palm of a guest's hand while returning their change can turn an 11% tip into an up to 18% tip!

That's a 7% jump just for reaching out and touching someone.

Because touching can be uncomfortable for some to do, here are some guidelines culled from research on the subject:

1. Whether you are a male or female server, it is generally more beneficial to briefly contact guests of the female persuasion.

2. Touching generally increases the tips from younger guests rather than older guests.

3. Touch your guest *only* on the shoulder (while dropping a check), or on the hand (while returning change). Both areas are considered to be safe, public areas of the body and the accompanying actions provide a reason for and distraction from the brief contact.

"Happiness never decreases by being shared."

- Buddha

4. Keep your contact under two seconds. Short touches are far less intrusive.

5. Relax, and be casual. A brief touch will communicate friendliness and humanity to your guest.

The key to being a Renegade and making more money is being seen as a person, not a food-fetcher.

Let Me Entertain You

Have you ever wondered why some bartenders make more money than servers working the same shifts in the same restaurants? Their product is cheaper, and therefore their check averages must be much lower... so how do they make those huge tips?

Bartenders have a unique position that better allows them to interact with their guests and create relationships. Bartenders are often the ones in the restaurant with the greatest "following" of devoted regulars. The secret to bartender success (and one easily applied at dining room tables) is simple: entertainment.

I'm not talking about the fancy, bottle-juggling, fire-breathing kind of bar entertainment or the "*eat*ertainment" of the singing waiter.

I'm talking about the easy kind of everyday entertainment that can subtly cause guests to see you as a real person and bond them to you.

Great bartenders tell jokes, leave riddles and

> **"You can't deny laughter. When it comes, it plops down in your favorite chair and stays as long as it wants."**
>
> - Stephen King
> *Renegade Author*

The key to being a Renegade and making more money is being seen as a person, not a food-fetcher.

> "The most expensive thing in a restaurant is an empty chair."
>
> - Jim Sullivan,
> *Renegade*
> *Restaurant Guru*

perform bar tricks. I will sit all night at a bar where the bartender has a few brain teasers and jokes to share with me. (Alright... I'll probably sit all night at just about *any* bar... but that's a whole other book).

Sharing a joke or a riddle with guests not only has the positive effect of entertaining them, it makes you stand out as an individual, and forms a sort of friendship.

 In a French study conducted by Nicholas Gueguen entitled "The Effects of a Joke on Tipping When Delivered at the Same Time as the Bill," in the *Journal of Applied Psychology*; the theory was put to test.

Servers were asked to give a card with a joke written on it to half of their guests and no joke to the other half. The study showed that guests who received a joke left 23% gratuity as opposed to 16% left by those who received no joke.

 That's a 7% increase for telling jokes!

The key to being a Renegade and making more money is being seen as a person, not a food-fetcher.

Rather than simply leaving a printed joke, I recommend:

1. Verbally tell a joke at the end of the meal. Choose one that is appropriate, non-offensive, and suits your personality and stick with it. You don't have to use a different one every time, just make it short and deliver it naturally. Riddles work especially well, as do knock-knock jokes.

2. Learn a couple of "brain teaser" puzzles that can be quickly set up with coins, matches or napkins. Set them up on the table, and see how long it takes for your guests to cave in and ask for the solution.

For some great jokes, brain teasers and bar tricks to share with your guests, check out bar-tricks.com and thatwasfunny.com! Also, download the free app "Bar Tricks" at the Apple App Store!

Obviously, you should steer clear of all comedy material that might be considered offensive (politics, religion, sex, and other material that couldn't be used onstage at a Bar Mitzvah should be avoided).

The Gift That Keeps On Giving

Have you ever had someone give you a gift or card at a holiday party and you haven't brought anything for them? If you're like most, you feel

The key to being a Renegade and making more money is being seen as a person, not a food-fetcher.

rotten and utter something like *"but... I didn't get you anything!"*

When presented with a gift, people feel a natural obligation to reciprocate.

See more ideas for small parting gifts to give you Guests in the "Quick Tips" section of this book.

You can turn this into better gratuities by offering your guests a little "something extra" as a gift. In fact, multiple scientific studies indicate that giving candies or mints to customers results in significantly larger tip percentages.

David Strohmetz and his colleagues Bruce Rind, Reed Fisher and Dr. Michael Lynn conducted a study on gift giving for the *Journal of Applied Social Psychology* entitled "Sweetening the Till: The Use of Candy to Increase Restaurant Tipping."

In their first study, they found that giving chocolates with the bill increased tips from 15% to 18%.

That's a 20% increase of the total tip!

The key to being a Renegade and making more money is being seen as a person, not a food-fetcher.

In a second study, where the server gave guests one piece of candy, then spontaneously offered a second piece, the average tip rose to 23% from 19%.

 That's an ADDITIONAL 21% tip increase!

A few pointers to make sure your gesture makes the maximum impact:

1. Buy and bring the candy yourself. Don't use the same kind that are sitting in the basket at the front door. You want this to clearly be a gift from you, not the restaurant (your increased tips will more than pay for the investment in a bag of Hershey's Mini's).

Invest in a bag of personalized candies that have your name on them, starting at 5¢ each at rushimprint.com!

2. Don't present the candies on the check tray. Drop the check, then take the candies out of your apron and place them in front of each guest. Again, the more you can personalize this gesture, the more credit you will get for it at tip time.

3. When you come back to pick up the credit card or go get change *make sure* to offer each guest another piece of candy. Don't just leave more candy on the table, verbally offer it.

The key to being a Renegade and making more money is being seen as a person, not a food-fetcher.

The whole point of becoming a *Renegade Server* is to distinguish yourself from other servers. In order to break away from the "process" that has become the American dining experience, you must seek out these small, genuine ways to connect with your guest.

If we're not in it together, then we're not in it to win it.

In the landscape of chain restaurants, similar menus, and formulaic training, it is easy to get lost and viewed as a cog in the restaurant machine.

Whether it's by wearing something distinct, telling a joke, or leaving a treat as a gift, you should strive to make your guests see you as an individual. *Renegades* get noticed.

New Tip $12.90

GUEST CHECK

2 Iced Tea	1.99
	1.99
2 Diet Cola	1.99
	1.99
Chix Caes	10.49
Burg/Fries	8.99
Ribs	13.49
Chix Pasta	12.29
tax	3.87
	57.09

Your 15% Tip ——— $8.56

Add 17% for Distinguishing Your Appearance ——— $1.71

Add 7% for Making Subtle Contact ——— $.59

Add 7% for Entertaining with a Joke ——— $.59

Add 20% for Giving Away Candies ——— $1.45

The key to being a Renegade and making more money is being seen as a person, not a food-fetcher.

SUMMARY

1. *A big, toothy smile leaves an impression.*

   Though it's easy to forget during a busy shift; a big, genuine, toothy smile is still the #1 tool of the *Renegade Server*.

2. *Make yourself physically distinct.*

   While it is important to come to work in a clean, pressed uniform, look for ways to stand out from the crowd.

3. *Make brief physical contact with your guest, if possible.*

   Like a handshake, a touch on the hand or shoulder communicates friendliness and safety.

4. *Entertain your guests with a joke or riddle.*

5. *Give small candies to your guests.*

   Giving treats to your guests prompts reciprocal giving on the tip line. The spontaneous offering of a second candy boosts tips even more.

Chapter 5:
Treat Me Like A Regular

Preview

1. By following the steps in previous chapters, you can increase your tips in relatively small increments. Now, you can increase those tips by increments of 100% by learning how to turn one visit into **multiple** visits.

2. Making a guest want to come back to your restaurant is especially valuable to you if they are coming back and specifically **asking for you**.

3. The best station in the world is the one filled with **your** friends, regulars and other industry professionals.

4. In this chapter, you will learn:

   - How to develop a loyal clientele of regulars by learning, remembering and using their names — and making sure they remember and use yours.

   - How to communicate to your guests that you are "their" server, and they should always ask for you.

   - How to attract other industry professionals to your station.

You want them to come back soon and often,
and <u>always</u> be looking for you.

Treat Me Like a Regular

Many of the ideas in this book will help you
increase your tip income bit by bit in a variety of
ways. Ten percent here, fifteen percent
there… it can add up to some big bucks!
The *BIG* win comes, however, by learning
how to increase your tips *100%* at a time.

The only way to *double* or *triple* your tips all
at once is to increase the number of visits your
guests make to your section. If you can turn one
visit into two… you have just doubled the amount
of tip revenue you have made from that guest. This
chapter suggests ways to turn casual diners into
devoted regulars.

"You have to
learn the rules
of the game…
then you
have to play
better than
everyone else."

- Albert Einstein
Renegade Physicist

Building Loyal Regulars

Wouldn't you agree that if your section was always
filled with regular customers and guests who had
requested to sit in *your* section, you would make A
LOT more money?

It always astounds me that most servers agree
that 'Regulars' are some of the best tippers in the

*You want them to come back soon and often,
and <u>always</u> be looking for you.*

**We always hear,
"Don't sweat the
small stuff," but
Renegade Servers
do sweat the
small stuff (so
their customers
don't have to).**

business, but few go out of their way to develop a regular clientele in the dining room. Many servers have simply resigned themselves to the idea that only bartenders can develop regulars. While the bar is a strong draw for repeat business and a hub of personality and activity, it is not the only place you will find regulars.

If you want to get your fair share of Regular business (and tips), you have only to figure out how to attract those regulars to yourself and your section.

The basic facts about Regulars are:

- People *first visit* restaurants because it is conveniently located or to try the food and drink.

- People *return* to restaurants based on the quality of their first visit.

- People *become regulars* at places where they have been made to feel important, special, and somehow better than the other guests. Where they feel they know the staff and the staff knows them.

- People *become frequent, super-regulars* at places that create a sense of belonging or community. That is, where they know the *other regulars*.

*You want them to come back soon and often,
and <u>always</u> be looking for you.*

The average guest's first visit is largely driven by some combination of marketing and location. Leave driving that *first* visit to the people in your company that develop advertising campaigns and promotions and who select restaurant sites. Your *real* goal, once they have made the first visit, is to make them want to come *back*.

Moreover, you want them to come back soon and often, and always be looking for <u>you</u>.

The following techniques are designed to help you endear yourself to your guests and create "business friendships" with them. Again, if your section was always filled with your "friends," wouldn't your tips immediately go through the roof?

Food always tastes better when someone else makes it.

The Name Game

What's in a Name? Big Money!
The famous business guru and motivational speaker, Dale Carnegie Jr. once observed that:

"A person's name is, to that person, the sweetest and most important sound in any language."

*You want them to come back soon and often,
and <u>always</u> be looking for you.*

The best section in the restaurant is one filled with your friends, family and guests who have requested you.

The best way to develop a regular clientele is to get to know your guests – and allow them to get to know you – *BY NAME.*

Every restaurant training guide in the world will surely, at some point, recommend that you introduce yourself to the guest. How many times have we all said or heard:

"Hi, my name is Edgar, and I'll be helping you today."

Or

"Here you go… one bacon cheeseburger. By the way, my name's Edgar. If you guys need anything else, just holler…"

While both of these old stand-bys get the job done, neither really connects you personally to the guest.

Remember the theme song from the old TV sitcom, "Cheers?" The famous lyrics about the neighborhood hangout crowded with regulars say:

*"Sometimes you want to go,
where everybody knows your name…"*

You want them to come back soon and often, and <u>always</u> be looking for you.

Those lyrics touch upon a very important but often neglected point. The whole point of me being a "Regular" is that people know *my* name.

Knowing the name of my server or bartender is good and important, but it does not make me feel like a *Regular*.

To develop a unique relationship and draw a regular clientele you must get your *guest's* name.

Remember, in order to become a Regular, the guest must feel:

- important
- special
- better than other guests

Of course, it's not always appropriate to ask for every guest's first name. There are really only a few naturally occurring situations that present comfortable opportunities to get your guest's name.

Start building your regular clientele by getting the *basics* right. Learn how to prevent common service mistakes in the "Quick Tips" section at the back of this book.

In order of frequency, they are:

- Thank You
- Host Seating
- Kids
- Return / Remember

You want them to come back soon and often,
and <u>always</u> be looking for you.

Thank You

Much research has been done indicating that a person is more likely to remember an interaction if his name was used at some point during its course. Moreover, people have been found to remember more facts about a given interaction the *more frequently* their names were used.

The easiest, most naturally occurring opportunity to get your customers' names is when you are presenting their change or charge slip and thanking them for their business.

These days it's typical for people to pay their restaurant and bar tabs with credit cards. The easiest way to obtain a guest's name is to simply read it off of her credit card.

Beware of "Superficial Congeniality"... acting fake-friendly instead of sincere-friendly.

When someone has given you that easy opportunity, you should always take advantage of it by using the name when thanking the guest. It is the first and easiest way to increase your tips!

*You want them to come back soon and often,
and <u>always</u> be looking for you.*

In her study, "Tipping Tips: The Effects of Personalization on Restaurant Gratuity," Karen M. Rodriguez found that servers could easily increase their tip percentages by using their guests' names when presenting the check.

Her study involved only guests who paid using a credit card at several different restaurants. Servers were randomly assigned situations where they were either to thank the guest using the name on the credit card or thank the guest using no name at all.

The amount of interest someone shows in you is likely to be directly proportionate to the amount of interest they think you are showing in them.

You may be surprised to learn that servers who dropped checks and said "Thank you very much, Mr. Smith," made 10% more in tips than servers who just said "Thank you very much."

That's a 10% raise in your income just for using two words!

Host Seating

The second most frequent and naturally occurring time for a guest to give you his name is at the host

*You want them to come back soon and often,
and <u>always</u> be looking for you.*

or greeter stand. When guests approach the host stand, they are prepared to give a party name as a condition of being seated. Although most restaurants only typically take guest names when there is a wait for tables, I suggest that your hosts ask for a party name for all guests. Guests will give their names naturally and happily even if they are seated immediately. It is perfectly natural, when your guests first enter the restaurant, for the hostess to say:

It is not enough to simply tell guests your name.

To truly make an impression, you should learn, remember and use their names.

"Hi! Welcome to Barney's. How many of you for dinner tonight? Two? Great. May I have a name for your party please?"

At this point, the guest will gladly give a name, expecting a short wait. It could only be a nice surprise when the hostess says:

"Excellent, Mr. Smith, we can seat you immediately in the dining room. Right this way please!"

By getting that small piece of information from your greeter or host, you can make a big impression! Upon being seated, simply make contact with the greeter and ask to share the party name with you.

You want them to come back soon and often,
and <u>always</u> be looking for you.

Now, upon approaching the table, you can introduce yourself using the party name:

"Welcome to Barney's. My name is Roger... how is the Smith party this evening?"

By simply adding the name of the party, you have already begun to develop the "business friendship" that will ultimately create regulars and earn you exponentially better tips!

When thanking your guests, always look them directly in the eyes.

Instead of just saying "Thanks, guys," say "Thank you for your business."

Kids

The server relationship with children at the table is naturally more casual than with the adults. While it is not always appropriate to approach a table and ask for the first names of all the grown-ups at a table, it is almost always O.K. to engage the kids.

A simple "Hi! I'm Sara, what's your name?" is a great way to engage young children at a table and make them feel like a more important diner. It also has the beneficial effect of bonding the parents to you. Parents feel a natural pride when their children

*You want them to come back soon and often,
and <u>always</u> be looking for you.*

interact well with others. Try introducing yourself to a young child at one of your tables and observe the adoring, proud gaze the parent gives their kid while answering.

During most family dining experiences, the kid is the *most* important VIP at the table. Once you ask the child to introduce himself, use his first name at every opportunity and watch your tips grow! Parents will thank you for engaging their children and, by doing so, making their own dining experience more harmonious.

Certain studies have shown that presenting guest checks on trays emblazoned with credit card logos can sometimes subliminally prompt an increase in tip!

ALERT – *Although using names is a powerful, positive tool, beware of falling into "False Familiarity." False Familiarity is when a server takes it upon herself to become too "jokey" or casual with her guests.*

Guests want to be made to feel comfortable, but there is always a line to be crossed. Do not get too involved with personal conversations, or ask for information that may be considered too personal. While it is O.K. to ask a child her name (or even how old she is), any good parent would become

You want them to come back soon and often,
and <u>always</u> be looking for you.

uncomfortable if you asked for too much
personal information from their child or
any member of the party. Be friendly, not
too familiar.

Return / Remember

Situations involving the return of a guest and remembering prior visits are the gold standard for developing regulars. They are also the hardest to come by and involve the most effort from the server. Though they are a little more involved than the situations mentioned previously in this chapter, the following techniques provide *much higher returns on the tip line*!

Keep an eye out for repeat guests. If you can recognize a guest that has been in your restaurant (and in your section), you will amaze them, and bond them to you. In essence, you will become "their server."

Recognizing a return guest is probably the hardest technique recommended in this book, as it requires you to pay scrupulous attention and take risks.

See if you can get your host or greeter to find out if your guests are in for the first time. If so, ask the greeter to leave you a signal like a coaster or napkin on the end of the table.

Now, when you approach, mention that you understand it is their first time in and ask if they would like extra help with the menu.

*You want them to come back soon and often,
and <u>always</u> be looking for you.*

Obviously, unless you have a catalog-like, "Rain Man", photographic memory (in which case, I advise you to immediately quit your serving job, move to Vegas and begin counting cards), you will not be able to remember every guest you have and recognize them should they ever come back into your restaurant.

Keep a couple packets of saltine crackers in your apron just in case you get a party with a young child.

Parents often appreciate having some food to occupy their toddlers right away, leaving them free to better peruse your menu.

Acquiring a knack for recognizing guests can be done gradually by using these techniques:

1. **Make the guest stand out in your mind** – Using key phrases to reinforce guests' identities can be done by practicing myriad techniques. A good, basic technique is one already mentioned in this chapter: Thank the guest by name. If you thank your guests by the names on their credit cards, they are much more likely to stick in your mind as individuals. Attaching real names to your guests prevents them from just becoming part of the shift-blur around you. You may even get lucky, and they will have such an unusual name that you would never forget it.

"Thank you very much, Mr. Tipsamillion! Make sure to ask for me when you come back!"

You want them to come back soon and often,
and <u>always</u> be looking for you.

2. **Take Risks** – If you have reason to think the guest
    has been in before, put it out there! If you have a good
    feeling that you have served the guest before, go
    ahead and ask!

"Weren't you in for lunch last week?"

If you are right, you will make the guest feel
really important that you remembered and
appreciated his last visit. If you are wrong,
it is a great way to create a conversation
regarding the regularity of his visits, and help you
match him with the right products.

Notice how the question was phrased to assume
a prior visit. Many servers do this to avoid embarrass-
ment. By saying *"You've been in before, haven't you?"* the
reply is always positive.

**For a list of
inexpensive items
you can keep in
your apron to wow
kids and their
parents, check out
the Quick Tips
section at the back
of this book.**

If you ask only *"have you ever been in before?"* You
might hear *"Only every Friday for the past two years…
and who might **you** be?"*

3. **Teamwork**—Two heads are better than one! If you
    think you recognize a guest, ask one of your teammates
    to help you recall the name.

You want them to come back soon and often,
and <u>always</u> be looking for you.

Invitations & Requests

These are the golden rules for developing a loyal regular clientele for yourself:

Make a list of the first names of any regulars you can remember and something special about them (where they work, their favorite seat, etc.)

Add one regular to your list every day.

1. If you want something, *ask for it.*

2. If you want people to return to your section, *invite them.*

3. If you want guests to *request* seating in your section, *request it of them.*

4. If you want to be remembered, *provide a memory.*

Once again, envision walking into your section knowing that most of the people seated there are your regulars, your friends, or had specifically requested for you to serve them. How much more money would you make from that section than from a section filled with strangers?

It has been my experience that there is not much difference between the "good sections" and "bad sections" on a restaurant floor. I do think, however that the section described above would definitely be the best one in the restaurant, and the good news is you can create it no matter which tables you have been assigned.

*You want them to come back soon and often,
and <u>always</u> be looking for you.*

1. **Invite your guests to return** – At the end of the
   meal, when returning your guest's credit card
   slip or change, make sure to invite them to
   come back. When you do this, it is very
   important that you do not use the following
   phrase:

   "Come back and see us..."

   This phrase is so common it has become meaningless
   to your guests. Everybody says it and too few mean it.
   It is the tool of the average food-fetcher, not the
   Renegade Server. A proper invitation has a real,
   personal touch and offers specific details. Something
   along the lines of:

   *"I see you liked your Chicken Fried Chicken!
   You should come back on Thursday, when it's
   always on special."*

2. **Make sure you ask your guest for their personal
   requests!** Many people would never think to request a
   particular server at a restaurant because no one has ever
   made it seem important. Ask all of your guests to
   request you during their next visit.

> **Make regular Guests
> stand out in your
> mind by associating
> them with a special
> characteristic.**
>
> **For example:
> "Mrs. Hyde likes
> Ranch on the side"
> or "Pete, Pete,
> works across
> the street."**

You want them to come back soon and often,
and <u>always</u> be looking for you.

"I had a great time serving you today, Ms Smith. My name's Tim, make sure to ask for me next time you come in!"

By asking them to request you *specifically*, you are building the ***business*** that is your section. You are also ensuring that on their next visit your guests will feel more important and be more confident in the quality of service they will receive. If they are confident that they will be treated like a VIP and receive great, personalized service, they are more likely to bring in friends and associates! That's more money for you!

One successful neighborhood bar & grill in Florida keeps a whiteboard in the back of the house where servers can record special facts about regulars, such as birthdays or special requests.

Love Notes

Communicating with your guests on a personal level is the key to developing regulars. That personal touch is not just demonstrated by your words and actions at the table, but long after the guest leaves your restaurant.

Treat your section of the restaurant as your own small business. Consider that, in order to be truly successful, every business must do some marketing and advertising. Take your cues from successful

*You want them to come back soon and often,
and <u>always</u> be looking for you.*

businesses around you and do some aggressive marketing of yourself and your section! Some of the best marketing tools I have seen in the past few years involve simple, yet creative ways of getting one's name into the hands of the customer.

To develop a strong clientele of loyal regulars, it is important to invite them back.

Make sure you always stress that they should *ask for you* when they return.

My favorite Chinese restaurant makes sure they are the only ones I call when I am craving Sesame Chicken. By leaving a refrigerator magnet with their name and phone number inside my order, they give me a handy tool to keep their information in sight. Unlike the phone book, search engine or yelp page, there are no other restaurants competing with them on my fridge.

Where I live, we have a scheduled, monthly street-sweeping on my side of the block. Anyone left parked on the side scheduled for cleaning faces a $35 violation (I have collected many). Recently, the day before sweeping, a local real estate agent has put a reminder note under the windshield-wipers of all the cars on my side of the block. More than once, his notes have reminded me to park on the opposite side of the street, thereby saving me an expensive ticket. I will certainly remember his name if I ever sell my house.

*You want them to come back soon and often,
and <u>always</u> be looking for you.*

These are both great examples of getting one's name into the customer's hands. There are many ways you can get *your* name to your guest and ask them to request you on their next visit.

1. **Write "Thank You" Notes** — Writing "thank you," along with your name on the guest's check or receipt has the beneficial effect of both personalizing your service and giving the guest your name so that they can request you as "their server." In addition to repeat business, scientific studies indicate that writing "thank you" notes can actually increase your tip on the current visit! Written expressions of gratitude have been shown to encourage guests to leave bigger tips.

In their study published in the *Journal of Applied Psychology*, entitled "Effect of Server's 'Thank You' and Personalization on Restaurant Tipping," Bruce Rind and Prashant Bordia studied a dining room server who randomly signed "thank you" notes on a percentage of her guest checks. The result was that she consistently received a tip increase of nearly 13% on the signed checks.

*You want them to come back soon and often,
and <u>always</u> be looking for you.*

*That is another immediate 13% in-
crease in your income, just by writing
"thank-you" and your name!*

2. **Write your name on the credit card voucher –**
When presenting your guests' credit card
vouchers, make sure to write your first name
on *their* copy. Just so they understand your
intention, make sure to pair it with an
invitation:

*"It was a pleasure serving you today,
Ms. Johnson. I wrote my name on your
copy so that you can <u>ask for me next
time you come in</u>."*

This is also a great way to distinguish the restaurant's
copy of the voucher from the guest's. Much better than
"The top copy's mine!"

**Look for ways
to write down
your name and
get it into the
guest's hands.**

**Notes that make
it into their
wallets or purses
are often most
successful.**

3. **Turn "To-Go" boxes into "Come-Back" boxes –**
by writing on them.

• Another opportunity to get your name in front
of guests is by using to-go boxes and bags. When

You want them to come back soon and often,
and <u>always</u> be looking for you.

you box up the guest's leftover food, write notes on the boxes. If your restaurant requires you to let the guest transfer their own food into a box, write your name on the bag.

- If you know the names of the guests (especially kids), write their names on each of the boxes, so they know what's what and whose is whose.

- If you don't know the guest's name, write what's in the box.

In studies of exceptional salespeople, the number one characteristic they all share is that they think and act differently than their less successful colleagues.

- Write a "thank you" note on the *outside* of the box that includes your name. Make sure to point it out by saying, "I wrote my name on your box, so you can ask for ___**me**___ next time you come in!"

- Write the date of the visit, so guests will know how long they have had the food in the fridge (or perhaps suggest an "expiration date" or even microwave instructions).

- Some servers have had great success by writing playful messages such as "Do Not Leave in Car" on the outside of the bag.

- Make sure to include special service items such as

*You want them to come back soon and often,
and <u>always</u> be looking for you.*

plastic silverware, napkins or wet-naps in the bag. Try arranging the food in an appetizing way in the box and freshening up the garnish.

4. **Give out "your card"** – Although a server is not expected to have a business card, there are other ways of getting your name and restaurant information into the guest's wallet or handbag.

My favorite technique is to grab one of the Manager-on-Duty's cards from the host stand, turn it over, and write your first name on the back. Now you have a personalized business card to give your guest, making it easier to <u>ask for you on their next visit</u>. Simply drop it off with the guest's change or credit card voucher and say something like:

For some more great ideas on how to sell more desserts, see the Quick Tips section in the back of this book.

"*I had a great time serving you today, Mr. Smith. We hope to see you again soon, and I wrote down my name so you can remember to <u>ask for me next time you come in</u>!*"

No matter which approach or combination you use, the result is the same: *instant regular!*

You want them to come back soon and often,
and <u>always</u> be looking for you.

Introductions

In addition to you knowing your guest, and your guest knowing you, there is another level to guest introduction that can help drive them to "Super Regular" status. Remember that the way to develop regulars is to make them feel special, important, and a member of your restaurant "community."

Try introducing your guests...

You can't choose your customers, but you can choose how you react and respond to them.

1. **To each other...** One of the best ways to make a guest feel like a regular, and to feel "membership" is to make sure that they know other regulars in your restaurant. In addition to introducing yourself to your guests, you should introduce guests to each other. Especially in a bar or neighborhood restaurant situation, guests go out for some sort of social interaction. By introducing guests to each other, you achieve several desirable results:

- Your guests stay longer (and spend more) because they become involved in conversation with others.

You want them to come back soon and often,
and <u>always</u> be looking for you.

- Your guests visit more frequently because they develop a social connection to your restaurant.

- Your guests require less personal attention from you, as they are being entertained by others.

These techniques work especially well in the bar and with single, "one-top" guests!

2. **To your Managers...** Introducing your managers to your guests is not only a great way to develop regulars and make your guest feel important... it can also be a great form of self-promotion! When you introduce your guest to your managers:

Scan this code to see how introducing your managers to your Guests can make you real money!

- Your guest feels extra important because they "know the manager."

- Your manager recognizes that you are doing a great job at connecting with your guests.

- Your value to your managers goes up, as any guest you introduce to a manager will inevitably say good things about you and your service. Happy managers stay out of your hair!

You want them to come back soon and often,
and <u>always</u> be looking for you.

Creating "Short-Term" Regulars

Finding out who your guests are and where they're from can achieve unexpected results. If your restaurant is near a hotel or convention center, or in a part of town where tourists and visitors frequent, you have an opportunity to develop "Short-Term Regulars."

If you were a tourist in your own city and had only one night to spend on the town, what would you do?

Jot down an answer for each night of the week.

Like many people, I travel frequently for my job. For many business travelers, being alone in an unfamiliar city can be a pretty boring situation. Although everything is new and potentially exciting, it's hard to know *where* to go and there is no one with whom to hang out. Doing anything by one's self is always less fun. Not knowing anyone takes that very important *social* aspect away from the dining and drinking experience.

If I only knew a few people in a city, I would probably spend most of my free time around those people.

This situation is extremely common for business travelers and small groups of tourists.

*You want them to come back soon and often,
and <u>always</u> be looking for you.*

Travelers are very easy to develop into regulars,
because they have a limited amount of time to get
to know your city and usually know no one else. If
you and others in your restaurant become
the only people a traveler knows in town,
he will eat every meal in your place.

If you find out that a guest is a visitor from
out of town, you should immediately go into
introduction overdrive. Use all of the techniques
above (introduce yourself, your manager and other
regulars), and make sure he gets your name right.
Write it on the back of a business card, and say
what shifts you work.

**People staying
in hotels (for work
or vacation) eat
virtually all of
their meals in
restaurants.**

**Do everything you
can to make sure
they do so mostly
in *yours*.**

In addition, make sure to introduce the guest to a
couple of bartenders.

That guest is guaranteed to spend the majority of
his time (and money) in your restaurant and, specifically, your section during the remainder of his
stay. You have become the only "community" to
which he has a connection while on the road.

Using these techniques to gain "Short-Term"
regulars also has the unexpected benefit of

*You want them to come back soon and often,
and <u>always</u> be looking for you.*

making sure that guest will come in to see you
(to TIP you) on future trips back to your town,
or recommend you by name to friends planning
a visit!

Driving More Industry Guests

Developing a strong following of "industry people"
is not that different from building a core group
of regulars.

Much like regular guests, industry folks
generally frequent the same places and go
where there is someone working whom
they know and who knows them.

**Some research
has indicated that
drawing a "smiley
face" on guest
checks increases
tips for female
servers, but
<u>decreases</u> tips for
male servers!**

Think of the last time you were with fellow
restaurant workers trying to decide where to go
get a drink after work. Doesn't someone inevitably
ask the question *"Where do we know someone
that's working tonight?"* Imagine if your name was
always the answer to that question.

A section filled with hospitality folks? Surely, you
would bathe in cash.

*You want them to come back soon and often,
and <u>always</u> be looking for you.*

In order to develop a strong Industry clientele, you should:

1. **Adjust Your Timing**
2. **Work the Circuit**
3. **Invest in the Industry**

1. Adjust Your Timing

If you want to cater to more restaurant and hospitality industry pros, you have a great model from whom you should take clues... *you!* To find the times when you are most likely to serve other restaurant folks, think of the times you are most likely to be out – and then work those shifts. Although they may seem counter-intuitive at first, these pointers will bring you tons more tips (if not free time).

> **Never use 'I'm in the business...' as a justification when complaining about someone else's service.**

- **CLOSE!** – Servers and bartenders go out together after work. In my experience, they always go out in groups and gather at the place that serves the latest. Happy is the server or bartender that is the last one left on the floor, for they are the ones who receive the monumental tips from their comrades who got off early! If you have a choice of whether to get cut an hour early or to close... choose the late shift. Servers and bar-

*You want them to come back soon and often,
and <u>always</u> be looking for you.*

tenders do their dining and drinking last, and the last server standing is the one who makes all of those generous tips (well worth the extra hour or two).

- **Happy Campers** – When working the close shift, be more tolerant of "campers." Service employees use their late-night dining and drinking sessions to catch up with each other, unwind and, of course, gossip. Make sure that you are making them comfortable rather than rushing them out the door. If you provide a spot in your section that is a comfortable late-night hang out, you will develop a steady clientele of servers and bartenders.

Remember that service industry people usually get to eat, drink and party last.

Do what you can to make sure you are the one <u>working</u> those times.

2. Work the Circuit

In every town, there are certain places where service folks hang out. Many restaurants and bars even offer "S.I.N." (Service Industry Night) or "H.I.P." (Hospitality Industry Professionals) or "F.B.I" (Food & Beverage Industry) nights with discounts and drink specials. Often, this practice even results in the existence of a "circuit" of sorts... where service pros hang out at different places on different nights of the week.

- **Be There** – When you figure out the circuit, work it. Go to S.I.N. nights and make sure to introduce yourself around. This is building your "brand" through networking.

*You want them to come back soon and often,
and <u>always</u> be looking for you.*

- **Use "Hand-Outs"** — Most restaurants have marketing materials called "bounce-backs", that is coupons or cards that are used to attract guests back into their restaurants. If available, ask your manager if you can have some of them. Write your first name on them and make sure to carry them with you in your purse or wallet. When out to dine, drink or party, leave a few bounce-backs with your server or bartender, encouraging them to use the discount in your restaurant and to <u>*ask for you*</u>.

3. Invest in the Industry

Everyone knows the old saying "you have to spend money to make money." It is especially true in the Service Industry. The reason hospitality workers are such great tippers is that they are investing in good tip returns or "tip karma." You should do the same.

> **When you get off shift, try to relax and grab a bite in a restaurant or bar other than the one you work in.**
>
> **It gives you a chance to interact with more industry pros and drive them into your section.**

- **Be a Good Tipper** — It should go without saying that tipping well when you are out will breed good tips when you serve. Although it is easy for serving professionals to be extra critical of service (as servers we tend to notice service mistakes far more easily), you should always tip well. Don't withhold tips for a bad experience; tip well and speak to a manager. That way, you get credit for being a good tipper *and* solve the problem.

You want them to come back soon and often,
and <u>always</u> be looking for you.

To make sure
her section was
the favorite for
local servers
and bartenders
getting off shift,
one industrious
server I know
always supplied
paper clips,
rubber bands
and coin rollers
at her tables.
She made
it easy for
them to count
their tips (and
counted a lot
more herself!).

- **Change the "Hook-Up"** – There is a perception out there that the reason hospitality workers tip so well is because we get "hooked-up" with free drinks and food. Not so. Hospitality pros tip well because we have empathy for hard work. There is actually a real danger in giving away free food & drinks to restaurant employees:

  - It reduces the perceived value of your product and your service (if it's so valuable… how can it be free?).

  - It can form bad habits in your industry guests, where they will tip you big this time for "comping" something, but tip far less whenever you don't.

If you really want to buy someone a drink as a professional courtesy or to return a favor, do this… *really buy it!* Yep, *buy it.* Walk over to the bar (in view of your guest), and <u>*pay cash for their drink*</u>. That way, it exponentially increases the value of your gesture, and that will translate to a much larger tip. You will find that this is one seed that reaps an enormous harvest!

*You want them to come back soon and often,
and <u>always</u> be looking for you.*

New Tip
$10.53

GUEST CHECK

2 Iced Tea	1.99
	1.99
2 Diet Cola	1.99
	1.99
Chix Caes	10.49
Burg/Fries	8.99
Ribs	13.49
Chix Pasta	12.29
tax	3.87
	57.09

Thank You!
Tina

Your 15% Tip ——— $8.56

Increase 10% for Saying "Thank You"
and Guest Name ——————— $8.6

Increase 13% for Writing "Thank You"
and Your Name on Check ——————— $1.11

You want them to come back soon and often,
and <u>always</u> be looking for you.

*You want them to come back soon and often,
and <u>always</u> be looking for you.*

SUMMARY

1. *Learn, use and remember your guests' names.*

   - Use guests' names when thanking them.
   - Make sure to write "thank you" and your name on their check.
   - Make children your VIP guests, and make sure to personalize their experience by using their first names.

2. *Make the guest your regular by inviting them back, and asking them to request your section.*

   - Always give the guest your name, and tell them to ask for you on their next visit.
   - Write your name on business cards, to-go food and credit card slips, so they won't forget that you are "their" server.
   - Introduce guests to bartenders, managers and each other, so they feel like regulars.
   - If you can turn 1 guest visit into 2, you have effectively *doubled* your income!

THE RENEGADE SERVER

"Uncommon strategies for making more money."

SUMMARY

Few of the ideas expressed in the preceding chapters are groundbreaking or revolutionary. In fact, most are not. The vast majority are just great steps developed by other servers in their genuine quests to make more money at their jobs without investing any more time.

As a professional server, you probably already use some or many of these tools. It is my hope that you will be exposed to a few new tricks and be able to combine them with your own.

Most importantly, combine them to become a *Renegade*. Rebel against the common, conveyor belt-like process of the modern dining experience. Make *yourself* the product. Club Sandwiches are on seemingly every menu in America, but there is only one **you**. Shake up your guests' dulled expectations and look for ways to engage, surprise and delight them at every turn. It is only by finding out what is special and unique about each guest and their expectations that you can deliver and stand apart from those around you.

Remember that TIPS no longer stands for "*To Insure Prompt Service.*" For the *Renegade Server*, it means:

"Uncommon strategies for making more money."

T — Treat Me Like a Regular

Learn , use and remember your guests names and make it important that they know yours and *ask for you.*

I — Increase My Check

Use unique language and timing to communicate choices to your guests at just the right moment.

P — Personalize My Service

Take the experience order first. Realize that guests come into our restaurants for their reasons, not ours. A successful *Renegade Server* accurately determines what the guest really wants, then delivers in abundance.

S — Stand Out

Don't come across as a cog in the "chain restaurant machine." Find small, real ways to make your guests see you for what you are — another person who genuinely cares about their individual experiences.

Using these new rules to earn gratuities, you will distinguish yourself and explode your tip-earning potential. Be a *Renegade* among food-fetchers, and guests will flock to your section and pay a premium for the privilege.

"Uncommon strategies for making more money."

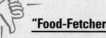

"Food-Fetchers"

Renegade Servers

"Food-Fetchers"	Renegade Servers
Serve food	Create just the experience the guest is seeking
Know the menu well enough to ring in orders	Know the menu well enough to confidently suggest things their guests will love
Work a section	Manage their section, So that **it** works for **them**
Are "seated" by the host	Have the host manage their wait lists of regulars & requests
Take Orders	Make memories
Are interchangeable	Are **irreplaceable**

Finally, I implore you to use these techniques every day, every shift. Let the 'food-fetchers' show up and sleepwalk through their shifts. A *Renegade* knows that there is one major reason to show up for work: *to have fun making money*. These techniques will help you do just that, but you must practice them consistently. Well done is better than "Well said," and excellence never gets boring.

Consider the professional baseball player. To reach the elite heights of the Major Leagues takes years of training, practice and a comprehensive knowledge of

"Uncommon strategies for making more money."

the game. Most pro ball players have been at it from a very young age. There are probably very few spring or summer days that were not spent on the baseball diamond practicing and working out. Still, even though they have spent the greater part of their lives playing the same game, running the same drills and practicing the same skills day after day, these things never become boring. They are exercises to keep them always at their best.

You should treat each shift the way the ball player approaches every game. Although you may work in the same restaurant five (or more) days a week, strive to live in the moment and make those shifts count. Even if hospitality is not your ultimate career goal, you owe it to yourself to make the time you <u>do</u> spend in the business pay the highest dividends. Become an expert at it; squeeze every dollar out of it you can.

Take the pointers in this book and apply them a couple at a time. Most of them, you will have to do routinely before they pay off. Remember, the pro athlete does not become strong after just one day in the gym or having done only one set of exercises. Like a workout, these techniques will only pay off and give noticeable results when applied consistently and routinely.

How the changing perceptions of good service may be shrinking your tips

Find the techniques that feel the most comfortable and best suit your service style and personality. Use them and hone them and make them your own. Soon, you will notice that you are enjoying more success and attracting bigger tips You will break away from the common, everyday service of the food-fetcher. You will become a *Renegade Server*.

A Word about "Bad Tips"

In the years since the first publication of *The Renegade Server*, I've had the honor of meeting and speaking with thousands of hospitality professionals. Many relate how they have taken the techniques and philosophies written about here and applied them to their own work. Some with amazing results. I've spoken with countless servers and bartenders who've related stories of tip incomes that have doubled and more... many of whom make six figures every year working the same hours as they did before.

One of the most frequently asked questions I encounter, however, is what to do about the "Bad Tipper." Some servers have said things like, "I tried the things in your book, and I still got stiffed on a tip last night!" The sad fact is that, no matter what you do or what training you receive, book you read, who you are or how you serve, there will always be times when you receive a "bad tip." Even if you do everything right, the eventuality of a "bad tip" is beyond your control. When it comes to a "bad tip," the only thing you control is how you respond.

I believe there are no such things as "Bad Tips" (or Bad Tippers). Tips can be big and small, but no gratuity is ever "bad," or taken for granted by the *Renegade*.

I'm reminded of a story a server was telling me about a regular customer who came into her restaurant several times a week. Because this customer was a straight 10% tipper, the servers working when he came in always tried to get out of serving him. Eventually, though, everybody occasionally got 'stuck' with this low-tipping regular and grumbled about how they never made 'good money' on him.

I advised this server that there was a way to make good money on that loyal regular. Instead of dreading his visit and trying to get out of serving him, she needed to make sure that only she - and no one else - served him every time he came in. The reason? If you're only going to make a small amount, the only way to turn that into 'good money' is to make it often. If I had a magic box that spit out $110 dollars every time I put a $100 bill in it, I would spend all my time shoving C-notes into that thing and throw rocks at anyone else that tried to come near it. At the end of the week, she will have made 30-40% on that frequent guest with a little more work. That's how to turn a 'bad tip' into big money. Work.

We all show up for each shift with a finite amount of 'emotional currency.' Meaning, there is only so much you can give and so much you can take in one day. You choose how that emotional currency is spent, invested or squandered. The crucial question for the *Renegade Server* throughout their shift is "how will I deploy my emotional currency in this moment?" If you get bummed out, infuriated, sidetracked or derailed by a low tip amount, remember that wasting your emotional currency on that fleeting situation will take away valuable time, attention and positive emotional currency you could be investing in the next (potentially big-tipping) Guest or party.

Thank you very much for your purchase of this book, and support of the *Renegade* philosophy. I'd love to hear how it works for you. Please send us your personal stories of *Renegade* service and results to **info@renegadehospitality.com**! Keep up with what others have to say at my blog space at **renegadehospitality.com**.

Tim Kirkland
CEO and Founder, Renegade Hospitality Group
renegadehospitality.com

BONUS SECTION

"Quick Tips for Making More"

*Apply one or all of these easy
techniques to stand out and delight your Guests!*

- *Acknowledge Birthdays*
- *Use Refillable Beverages to Increase Tips*
- *Keep Inexpensive Items in Your Apron for Kids*
- *Respond & Recover from a Service Mistake*
- *Prevent Service Mistakes*
- *How NOT to Respond to a Guest Complaint*
- *Subtly Influence Guest Behavior*
- *Sell More Wine*
- *Sell More Wine by the Bottle*
- *12 Little Ways to Show Care for Your Guests*
- *Serve Better and Sell More at Breakfast*
- *Sell More Desserts*
- *Take Care of Your Team*

BONUS SECTION

Acknowledge Birthdays

1. *Always* offer to take pictures when a camera is present.

2. Write (or have the kitchen write) the name of the guest of honor on the dessert plate in sauce or chocolate syrup.

3. Instead of singing *"Happy Birthday,"* whisper to the guest of honor that your "gift" will be to bypass this embarrassing ritual.

4. If they want you to sing, do it with flair. Sing it backwards (standing facing away from the table), or under water (with a glass of water above your head). Whatever you do, don't sing it slowly so that it sounds like a funeral march. Sing it briskly (half again as fast as you usually hear it).

5. If gifts are opened at the table, tie the bows onto the back of the guest of honor's seat.

6. "Name" a drink or shot after the guest of honor, and recommend it to the party.

7. At the beginning of the meal, upon finding out that it is a special occasion, ask the hosts if they'd like you to begin "chilling" a bottle of champagne or sparkling wine for later.

8. Keep a box of inexpensive, generic birthday cards in your arsenal. Sign one and present it with the check. This is a great way to turn a couple of quarters into a couple of bucks!

BONUS SECTION

How To Use Refillable Beverages To Increase Tips

Many guests' "Tip #" can be negatively affected by time. *The **number one** indicator of service timing for most guests is measured by drink refills. Make keeping glasses **full** your highest priority!*

1. For soft drinks, approach with a full glass to replace the glass they have. Never leave the guest without a beverage.

2. If refilling at the table, always pick up the glass and fill beside the table. Never reach or fill over the table top.

3. Before topping off a coffee cup, check with the guest. Adding uninvited coffee may upset the way they've mixed their cream and sugar. The same goes for iced tea.

4. When replacing or refilling diet cola or decaf coffee, softly say the word "diet" or "decaf" as you approach to let them know you remembered.

BONUS SECTION

Inexpensive Items To Keep In Your Apron For Kids

1. ***Crackers*** - for infants and toddlers, offering individually wrapped crackers to the parents at the beginning of the meal will be a welcomed distraction.

2. ***Crayons*** - if your restaurant doesn't already provide them, you should. Don't forget something to mark on. A page torn from a coloring book will do.

3. ***Small Magic Tricks*** or ***Puzzles***

4. ***Wet Naps*** - for faces, hands and other places

5. ***Candy*** - small lollipops and candies will leave a lasting impression with your little VIP's. They will always want to come visit you *in your section (make sure to check with parents before offering kids candy).*

6. ***Balloons*** - and other small toys (like plastic rings) are a welcome alternative to sweets for parents watching their kids' sugar intake. Make sure to quietly give the parents the option.

BONUS SECTION

How To Respond and Recover from a Service Mistake or Guest Complaint

1. ***Recognize*** - Identify the problem by listening to the guest completely. Recognize that it is indeed a problem and immediately apologize, saying something like *"I'm sorry about that. That's not how we usually do it."*

2. ***Remove*** - Immediately remove the offending dish or other item. Never leave it there while you resolve the problem. Out of sight, out of mind!

3. ***Resolve*** - Set the appropriate measures in motion to resolve the problem. This is the time to get the kitchen or manager working on the problem.

4. ***Replace*** - Always bring some food (like soup or a salad) to replace any dish you removed while the problem is solved. Leaving a guest with no food while others are eating only makes things worse.

5. ***Re-plate*** - Never just reheat or re-cook the item and send it out on the same plate. Send it out on a clean plate with fresh garnish and fresh, hot sides.

How NOT To Respond To A Guest Complaint

1. ***DO NOT*** - cite "*being busy*" as the reason for a problem. Being busy should be considered a result of success, not a reason for failure! For the average food-fetcher, being busy may be problematic and an excuse. For the *Renegade*, it means *more opportunity*. Remember, if you tell your guests that being busy is the problem, they might just *solve* that problem for you.

2. ***DO NOT*** - blame the guest's problem on another problem *(the truck didn't come in, our cook called in sick, the dishwasher is broken, etc...)*. You are basically turning one problem into two problems for the guest. The guest wants to know *how* you will *fix* it, not why it is *broken*. Never ruin an apology with an excuse.

3. ***DO NOT*** - indicate that a problem has happened before or is chronic. Indicating that a problem happens all the time will take away the guest's confidence in your ability to fix it. Always indicate that the problem is *rare and immediately solvable*.

BONUS SECTION

How Prevent Service Mistakes

1. **Repeat** - your guests' orders back *exactly* the way they say it to reassure them you heard any special requests.

2. **Write** - the order down *as you are repeating it*, so the guest has confidence you will get it right and ring it in correctly.

3. **Reinforce** - their choice by saying something like "excellent choice," or "that's the staff favorite."

4. **Double-Check** - the order once more at the POS before sending to the kitchen or bar.

5. **Announce** - the dishes as you serve them and set them on the table. Always use the full menu name and include any special modifications or requests (such as "one Smokehouse Cheddar Burger, medium-rare, hold the onions), so that the guest is assured they are getting it just the way they ordered it. Avoid using abbreviations and "auctioning" food (*"O.K., who had the burger?"*).

How To Subtly Influence Guest Behavior

1. ***The "Sullivan Nod"*** - Another industry contribution from restaurant consultant Jim Sullivan. Research indicates that as much as 70% of all communication is non-verbal. When suggesting items you want the guest to buy, slowly nod your head and smile. You are basically "framing" your suggestion with a positive gesture... one that the guest will usually mimic and then buy!

2. ***Think (and speak) Positively*** - Subconsciously, people tend to dismiss the first part of a negative sentence and remember the second. Everyone knows that when you tell a child *"Don't touch the stove,"* they only hear *"touch the stove."* Negative commands and phrases often work the same way for adults, so if you say "no problem" instead of *"my pleasure"* or *"you're welcome,"* you are basically introducing a <u>problem</u>. Make negative commands work for you by saying things like *"I don't have to tell you that **you have to try the cheesecake.**"*

BONUS SECTION

How To Sell More Wine

Because wine is typically priced higher than most other beverages in a restaurant, it can be a great way to increase the check totals on which you are tipped. Wine also helps make a meal more of an "experience" for the guest.

1. **Pair with Food** - Know which food items on your menu pair well with which wines and vice versa. Your chef and bartender will be able to help. Make a list with popular dishes on one side and your wine list on the other. Draw lines between them, so you can suggest dishes to go with what the guest is drinking, or wine to complement their chosen meal.

2. **Pair with Occasions** - a great way to sell wine is to attach it to good times, such as "this is a great lazy summer afternoon wine," or "this is a terrific celebration (or first date, anniversary, etc.) wine."

3. **Use Real Descriptors** - Unless you're dealing with a world-class wine aficionado, stay away from esoteric descriptors like "subtle," or "complex." Use words that communicate real flavors like *berries, citrus, apples* or *butter.*

BONUS SECTION

How To Sell More Wine by the Bottle

1. ***Rule of Thumb*** - Whenever two or more people are drinking the same type of wine, offer a bottle.

2. ***Cork n' Carry*** - These days, many States have what is called a "cork and carry" or "cork and go" law. Basically, this type of law allows guests who have purchased a bottle of wine in a restaurant to take any leftover wine home with them in the bottle.*

   The great thing about this law is it allows you to serve a bottle of wine in situations where it would otherwise be inappropriate or irresponsible.

   For example, if the guest's favorite wine is only available by the bottle, and not by the glass, you can recommend they buy the bottle and take the rest home to enjoy later. Another good example might be a single guest who is staying at a nearby hotel.

   * Ask your manager about cork and carry laws in your area, and how such transactions should be handled.

BONUS SECTION

12 Little Ways to Show _Care_ for our Guests

These small gestures are basic steps of etiquette that are often forgotten. Your guest will be impressed if you remember the "little things."

1. **Hold the Chair** - for a guest who is sitting down.

2. **Take the Coats** - for guests that have them. Hang them on hooks near their table or on the backs of their chairs. Don't just point out the hooks... _hang them up._

3. **Clean It** - When bringing service items to the table, always make a display of wiping them down with a clean cloth before leaving them. This technique is especially effective for high chairs or booster chairs and condiment sets.

4. **Do It Yourself** - When a guest has spilled and requests a towel to wipe up, make sure you do the wiping. Never just drop off a towel and let the guest do the dirty work.

12 Little Ways to Show *Care* for our Guests

5. ***Remove the Caps*** - of requested condiments. If a guest requests steak sauce, remove the cap and set it next to the bottle when you deliver it.

6. ***Offer the Paper*** - Single guests can get bored easily. Bring the daily newspaper to work with you every day, and offer it to one-tops that are seated in your section or solo Guests at your bar. It is a small investment that pays huge dividends.

7. ***Be aware*** - of the little things that could affect their visit. Is the air conditioner aimed right at their table (and their hot food)? Watch for signs that guests are unhappy with their environment, such as taking off or putting on sweaters and jackets and looking up at the ceiling at vents or fans.

8. ***Look Out for Lefty*** - Make it a point to notice who is left-handed at your tables. Replace silverware and napkins on the left and point mug handles to the left. Make sure to "get credit" for noticing by mentioning it.

BONUS SECTION

12 Little Ways to Show *Care* for our Guests

9. ***In the Restroom*** - If you use the same restroom as your guests, always wash your hands before leaving (even if you just went in to check out your make-up). The guest never knows why you are in there.

10. ***At the Sink*** - Offer the hand sink to the guest first. If you are there first, leave the water running for the guest and give them a couple of "courtesy pops" of the paper towel dispenser.

11. ***Be A Tour Guide*** - When a guest asks for directions to the restroom (bar, patio, pay phone, etc.), always walk them to their destination. Never point and describe directions.

12. ***Send a Pro*** - If a guest comments on something they are enjoying, send an expert to the table when possible. Guests love to speak to chefs about food, bartenders about exotic tequilas, or managers about how long the restaurant has been open.

Serve Better & Sell More at Breakfast

1. ***Juice Before Coffee*** - When seating guests for breakfast, offer to start them off with a glass of juice when the menus go down. Always offer juice before coffee. Because coffee is a refillable beverage, the person who drinks a glass of juice is likely to follow up with a cup of coffee if they still want something to drink. The guest who gets a bottomless cup of coffee first is less likely to purchase a second beverage.

2. ***Toast, Scones and Muffins*** - are the 'appetizers' of the breakfast menu. Everyone likes them, and they go with everything. Offer a guest an order of buttered toast and jam (as all sides of toast are) or a muffin or scone to "start on" while they look over the menu. Breakfast is the first meal of the day, and people come hungry. Why not get them started with a snack and beverage right when they sit down?

BONUS SECTION

Serve Better & Sell More at Breakfast

3. ***Side of Bacon*** - Breakfast meats have earned "guilty pleasure" status in these health-conscious times. Offer a side of bacon, sausage or ham for a couple to share.

4. ***Offer a Newspaper*** - to your Guests at breakfast. A small investment in a couple of papers each morning can translate into big bucks at tip time! Make sure to get credit by asking Guests if they'd like you to bring them a paper, rather than just leaving the papers out on the table.

5. ***Know Your Combos*** - so that you can point out better values to your guests as they build their breakfasts.

Sell More Desserts

1. ***Ask if the guest likes chocolate***, then make recommendations based on the answer. If the guest likes chocolate, describe in detail your best chocolate dessert. If the guest does not, describe your finest fruit pies or bread pudding. The great thing about this question is that it gives you an opportunity to describe a delicious dessert that you already know the guest will like. If all you ask is if anyone "saved room," you never even get to describe a dessert.

2. ***Focus on the "nutritional value"*** of dessert rather than things like fat, carbs and calories. The dairy cream and farm fresh eggs in your cakes also have tremendous value for their calcium and protein content. Carrot Cake counts as a vegetable. (All to be delivered tongue-in-cheek, of course).

3. ***Always offer coffee as a pick-me-up*** at the end of the meal. Guests who have entered "food coma" will often order coffee as a digestive aid. Coincidently, guests who are drinking coffee are twice as likely to then share a dessert.

4. ***Suggest that parents take a dessert*** home for the babysitter.

BONUS SECTION

Take Care of Your Team

Earn the reputation within your restaurant of being the best internal tipper.

Remember that the speed and quality of everything that arrives at your tables is influenced by a variety of other people. Especially in times of extreme need (like fixing a mistake or re-firing a meal), you want your support crew to be as motivated to help you as you are to help your guest.

Being the best tipper will give you the advantage. If you are required to tip a certain percentage to a teammate, always round up. For those you are not required to tip, pick up the occasional round of beers next time you are all out and praise the team member to your managers.

> **"At a car dealership, the person who sells the car is the hero, and also gets the commission. But if the mechanics don't service that car well, the customer won't return."**

- Roger Staubach

Build a Renegade Restaurant!

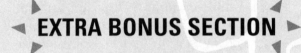

◄ EXTRA BONUS SECTION ►

for Managers,
Trainers & Supervisors

Use these tips to help your team continually learn
the value of salesmanship and hospitality and create
an environment where the server, the restaurant
and the guest all win!

Build a Renegade Restaurant!
Use **The Renegade Server** in your next

– Pre-Shift Huddle –
– All-Team Meeting –
– Manager Meeting –
– One-on-One Coaching Session –

Every week, choose one of the techniques
from this book to focus on with your team.
Use the following ideas to lead team meetings,
create one-on-one learning opportunities and
incentivize your staff to achieve higher sales,
bigger tips and better guest experiences!

Extra Bonus Section for Leaders

Tips to Build More Regulars

1. ***"Regular Concentration"*** - During your pre-shift huddle, stand in a circle facing in. Have one person start by stating the name of a regular guest that is likely to come in that shift. The next person then has to say something about that regular (like "*likes to sit at table 12*", or "*drinks Stoli Raz and Tonic,*" or "*wife's name is Sandy.*") No negative remarks allowed. The person who can't think of a something to add has to think of another name, and the game continues.

2. ***"Introduction Overdrive"*** - Tell your team that you want to spend most of the shift on the floor meeting guests. Encourage them to introduce you, by name, to as many regular and new customers as they can. Give prizes for most introductions, guest from farthest out of town, most kid introductions, etc.

3. ***"Profile Cards"*** - During a team meeting, provide cards so that everyone can write the name of their favorite regulars at the top of a card and list special things about that guest on it (favorite dish, birthday, kids' names…). Provide an index file in the back of the house where the cards can be stored (alphabetically by first name). Servers can use it as a reference if they see those guests

Extra Bonus Section for Leaders

sitting in their sections. Encourage your team to add to the profiles as they get to know each guest better.

4. *"Popularity Contest"* - Encourage servers to invite guests to return and to specifically ask for them. Get your Host or Greeter team to track how many times guests ask to be seated in a particular server's section. Post the results on your communication board, and give a prize (gas cards work great) to the server with the most requests accumulated every month.

5. *"Say My Name"* - Have your team brainstorm unique ways to find out a guest's name and use it and share it. For example, if a server obtains the guest's name from a credit card, he could share it with the Hostess, who can then thank them by name on their way out.

Tips to Teach Staff to Serve Better and Sell More

1. *"Change is Good"* - Bring a jar of coins into the meeting and ask the team how much your restaurant makes on every dollar. Once everyone has guessed, pull out a nickel and let them know that it is the national average. Then, pull out the

Extra Bonus Section for Leaders

amount of change that represents how much your restaurant currently takes to the bottom line. Finally, go around the room and solicit the amount each server believes they make in percentage tips. It will probably average out to between 15% and 20%. Pull that amount of change out and lay it next to the amount the restaurant makes. This is a great way to begin a conversation about tips being paid commissions on every dollar sold, and why it benefits the server to pump up their check averages.

2. ***"My Tip #"*** - Ask each member of the team the best way to make more tips. Write their answers on a flip chart (smile, be friendly, remember drinks, etc.). Now ask everyone what their "tip number" is. Write the average (like 15%) on the flip chart. Now ask the group if their 15% usual tip *includes* all of the behaviors on the board. This is a great way to begin a discussion about how tips are really primarily driven by check totals, and that the guest <u>assumes</u> good service in their usual tip.

3. ***"The French Fry Question"*** - Describe a common up-sell approach by talking about the use of the "French Fry" question described on page 82. Ask members of the group to identify other places and other industries they hear similar approaches (at the electronics store, the movies, etc.). Now,

Extra Bonus Section for Leaders

discuss alternate ways to suggest items to the guest BEFORE they have ordered.

4. ***"Restaurant Speak"*** - Using the list of common, tired restaurant phrases in Chapter 3, identify those that are used by the team and post them. Each day make one the "Focus Phrase." Each day, write the "Focus Phrase" ("*Can I get you something to drink?*" for example) on a board visible to the team, and discuss alternative phrases.

5. ***"High Sales Hold 'Em"*** - During the pre-shift meeting, let the group identify some great "add-on" type items from the menu that they like to sell, such as salads, premium cocktails, soups, juice, appetizers or desserts. Assign each item a playing card "value" (for example, "Fire House Nachos" = King of Hearts, "Chocolate Danger" = Ace of Spades, "Century Margarita" = Jack of Diamonds, etc.) and post the list. Put a deck of playing cards in your pocket, and let the team know that each time they sell one of the items, they can trade in a copy of the receipt for the corresponding card. The goal is to assemble poker hands by the end of the shift (or the end of the week). Assign each great hand a posted prize value (for example, a Full House is worth movie passes, three of a kind is worth a lottery ticket, two pair is worth five fewer roll-ups in their sidework, etc...).

Tips for Helping Servers "Read" Guests

1. *"**Who Am I?**"* - Before your team huddle, go through a few different magazines and pull out pictures of a wide variety of people in different social situations. During the meeting, hold each picture up one at a time and ask the group to invent a "back story" for each ("*They are a family on vacation*," or "*They are out on a date*," etc.). Now, based on the story the group invented, have everyone come up with ideas centered around the assumption that this pretend group is coming to dinner in your restaurant. Discuss what their experience expectations may be. Have the group identify things from the menu that they think may suit the "diners," what kinds of drinks they might like to hear about, and what their timing expectations may be based on the information the group has come up with.

2. *"**Recommendation Cards**"* - Using a stack of index cards, make "flash cards" for your menu items, so that the name of menu item is written on the front of one card. One by one, read the name of a menu item and elicit from the group what "kind" of guests usually like this item, and why. For example, you read off "Make Your Own

Extra Bonus Section for Leaders

Pizza," and the group may come up with "Kids love this because it is interactive, and they can be creative with their toppings, and — of course — it is cheesy pizza!" write all of their responses on the back of the card:

WHO — Kids
WHY — Interactive, creative, cheesy

A dish like "Seared Ahi Salad with Ginger-Soy Dressing" may elicit answers like:

WHO — Young ladies and Business Women at Lunch
WHY — Quick ticket time, cool, low-cal, low-fat, sweet and exotic

This exercise will help servers learn that they should tailor their recommendations. During another meeting, perform the card exercise backwards; that is, read the "Who" descriptors and "Why" they like it, and see if they can guess the dish.

3. *"First Timers and Old Timers"* - On a flip chart, divide the page into two columns, labeled "First Time Guests" and "Regulars." Now ask the group to come up with ideas of different things each group may need or want to know and how their expectations may differ (for example, First Time

Extra Bonus Section for Leaders

Guests may not know about a famous signature drink or where the restrooms are, whereas Regulars will want to know if there is anything new on the menu, or if there is a special).

4. ***"Time Keepers"*** - Each guest has a different expectation for the timing and pacing of the meal. Ask your team to come up with five different dining scenarios (business lunch, special occasions, etc.). Now ask how they think these situations may call for different speed of service and list different techniques for speeding up or slowing down the pace of a meal.

5. ***"A Moment of Silence"*** - Randomly, during the middle of a team huddle — preferably in mid-sentence — just stop talking and remain silent for 30 seconds. Point out that only 30 seconds seemed to take forever and relate it to how the guest must feel when waiting to be greeted, seated, served… etc.

Tips to Encourage Team Members to Stand Out as Individuals

1. ***"Getting to Know You"*** - When there is a new team member in the meeting, ask them to give a

Extra Bonus Section for Leaders

"group interview." Then go around the circle and allow each team member to ask a question about the new person that does not involve the restaurant, like "*Where did you go to school?*" or "*What do you do in your free time?*"

2. ***"One of These Things is Not Like the Others"*** - Brainstorm ways that each team member believes they make themselves distinct (either in appearance or personality) to their guests without violating the restaurants uniform dress code.

3. ***"Comedy Club"*** - Go around the circle and have each team member tell their favorite joke that would be appropriate to tell any guest.

4. ***"Different in a Good Way"*** - Choose five restaurants in your trade area and list them on a flip chart. Now have your team list 20 things that differentiate you from them, ***without*** using food, menu, price or facility as distinctions. Make sure answers are specific ("*Our people*" doesn't count, "*Our people know more about steaks*" does.) Post the list.

5. ***"Keep Going!"*** - For more ideas on meetings, games and team member incentives, log on to renegadehospitality.com!

Learn More. *Earn More.*

Renegade Server In-A-Box

***Renegade Server* In-A-Box** is the complete restaurant training system based on the book you hold in your hands. It is a comprehensive toolkit that will help trainers and managers train the sales and service skills from *The Renegade Server* to new employees and existing teams alike. It includes a print version of the book as well as:

***The Renegade Server* 3-CD Audiobook**
***The Renegade Server* LIVE 88 minute DVD** and a
CD-ROM which contains:

- Complete slide deck presentation that teaches the *Renegade* philosophy and tactics in an interactive classroom format

- Leader's Guide including step-by-step instruction for conducting the training

- Learner's Workbooks for trainees to capture and keep the lessons of *The Renegade Server*

- Classroom handouts and flashcards

- Meeting & incentive templates

- Much, much more! Visit ***Renegadehospitality.com*** for details.

THE RENEGADE SERVER

*Learn More. **Earn More.***

Live Seminars & Workshops

Find out why over 20,000 people attend Tim Kirkland's engaging and informative seminars every year!

Tim's delivery is professional, engaging and balanced with real-world experience and good-natured humor. Attendees are guaranteed to come away with dozens of real, immediately useable tools and tactics, not just 'inspiration' from the stage (*though there's plenty of that, too*). All of our content is intricately tailored for each client and designed to specifically address the goals, expectations, needs and culture of the organization.

Tim speaks with authority on a variety of subjects including Customer Service, Salesmanship, Leadership, Marketing, Change Management and Team Development.

> *"Tim presented a keynote address and two breakout sessions at our National Training Camp. His message was clear, concise, and completely in line with the message of our convention. Tim gave our audience members simple tactics that they could use right away to build their businesses. **By far, Tim was the best convention speaker I have seen** at any Buffalo Wild Wings convention."*
>
> **- Nikki Fuchs de Calderon**
> Director of Management Development,
> Buffalo Wild Wings

> *"Tim Kirkland allowed us the opportunity to wrap up our 2 ½ day franchisee convention in a powerful way. Tim understood our unique audience of corporate employees, franchisees and managers and was able to connect with them on a real level. We solicit feed-back from our attendees through an online survey after the event and **Tim Kirkland's ratings were the highest we've ever seen from a guest speaker.** I highly recommend Tim to your organization if you're looking for a high-energy, motivated speaker who can really connect with the audience and share a powerful message."*
>
> **- Heather Neary**
> Chief Marketing Officer, Auntie Anne's, Inc.

Learn More. *Earn More.*

The Renegade Server LIVE DVD

In this live version of the best-selling book, author Tim Kirkland brings his unique money-making insights to life with thought-provoking, real-life anecdotes, high-energy interactions and good-natured humor. Filmed live on stage during one of Tim's popular *Renegade* seminars, this is THE tool that helps servers and bartenders make more money while helping managers and owners train the skills that drive sales and intensify guest loyalty. Show it to your team today, and make more money tomorrow!

Tip Clips Digital DVD

This high-impact digital training tool takes uncommon insights from the best-selling book and brings them directly to the restaurant floor. Comprised of thirty-three, 1- to 4-minute-long digital video clips, this is the mobile training tool that will put the power of *The Renegade Server* in your team's hands every shift. The CD-ROM features Tim Kirkland communicating the most important parts of the book in both .mp4 and Quick Time file formats so you can train on any computer OR mobile device. PLUS – a second bonus Video DVD disc for use on the big screen! This set of powerful clips makes an invaluable addition to any restaurant training program.

Learn More. ***Earn More.***

The Renegade Server AudioBook

This is the 3-CD audio version of Tim Kirkland's bestselling book for full-service servers, bartenders and restaurant operators, read by the author. Use your travel time or exercise time to get smarter, faster and make more money.

Check out *The Renegade Server* Coaching Handbook

This supplement to *The Renegade Server* teaches managers how to implement the crucial lessons and tactics contained in the best-selling book in ways that front-line teams will value and adopt. It also extends the philosophies and strategies from the original book and applies them to the nature and function of leadership itself. Full of ideas, tools, meetings, incentives and discussion guides, this valuable addition will help you elevate not just your team's performance, but yours as a leader, as well.

References

Crusco, April H. and Christopher G. Wetzel, "The Midas Touch: The Effects of Interpersonal Touch on Restaurant Tipping," *Personality and Social Psychology Bulletin*

Garrity, Kimberly and Douglas Degelman, "Effect of Server Introduction on Restaurant Tipping," *Journal of Applied Social Psychology*

Gueguen, Nicholas, "The Effects of a Joke on Tipping When it is Delivered at the Same Time as the Bill," *Journal of Applied Social Psychology*

Rind, Bruce and Prashant Bordia, "Effect of Server's 'Thank You' and Personalization on Restaurant Tipping," *Journal of Applied Social Psychology*

Stillman, JeriJane W. and Wayne E. Hensley, "She Wore a Flower in Her Hair: The Effect of Ornamentation on Non-verbal Communication," *Journal of Applied Communication Research*

Strohmetz, David, Bruce Rind, Reed Fisher and Michael Lynn, "Sweetening the Till: The Use of Candy to Increase Restaurant Tipping," *Journal of Applied Social Psychology*

ABOUT THE AUTHOR

Tim Kirkland helps people make more money. He is a customer crusader.

As a best-selling author, consultant and speaker, Tim's books, training materials, seminars and other works are used by over 25,000 restaurants, hotels, retail locations and universities worldwide to train and inspire teams to sell more, serve better, lead passionately and succeed. Leading brands that use Tim's products and programs include Applebee's, Brinker International, Coca-Cola, Buffalo Wild Wings, Marriott, Kimpton, MillerCoors, Beam Global, Grease Monkey, Sodexo, Shamrock Foods, Auntie Anne's, Tim Horton's and hundreds more.

During his 25+ years in the hospitality industry, Tim has led training and marketing departments for numerous respected brands, been an award-winning operator and a successful restaurateur. His programs focus on specific, actionable tactics that increase sales and intensify guest loyalty by aligning the interests of the company, the crew, and the customer. He delivers highly customized presentations on customer service, salesmanship, marketing, leadership and team engagement.

Tim is an alumnus of the Harvard Kennedy School and CEO of Renegade Hospitality Group, which serves as a professional advisory resource to the restaurant, hotel, retail and customer service industries. You can reach him at **renegadehospitality.com**.

The Shift: How to
Plan It, Lead It, Make It Pay

will help every foodservice manager understand the architecture of the revenue-generating shift. They'll learn how to break down period goals to shift targets, the best practices related to leadership *before, during* and *after* the shift, how to coach each member through each shift, and how to make every customer interaction positive in the dining room, drive-through or counter. This 60-minute DVD is used in over 45,000 restaurants worldwide. Order online at Sullivision.com or Amazon.

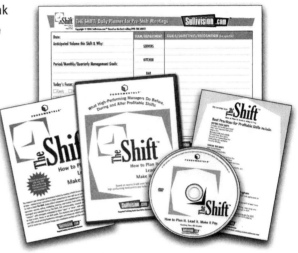

Buy Both & Save!
Jumpstart DVD
AND The Shift DVD

This Dynamic Duo of training DVDs are guaranteed to drive more revenue in any restaurant, every shift. Effective for both full-service and quick-service food service operations. Get them both for a great price at **Sullivision.com**

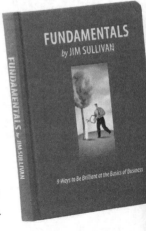

*Uncommon Strategies for Making More Money
in 21st Century Food Service*

*Uncommon Strategies for Making More Money
in 21st Century Food Service*

_____

_____

_____

_____

_____

_____

_____

_____

_____

_____

_____

_____

_____

_____

_____

_____

_____

_____

*Uncommon Strategies for Making More Money
in 21st Century Food Service*

*Uncommon Strategies for Making More Money
in 21st Century Food Service*

_____

_____

_____

_____

_____

_____

_____

_____

_____

_____

_____

_____

_____

_____

_____

_____

_____

_____

*Uncommon Strategies for Making More Money
in 21st Century Food Service*

NOTES

Uncommon Strategies for Making More Money
in 21st Century Food Service

NOTES

*Uncommon Strategies for Making More Money
in 21st Century Food Service*

_____

_____

_____

_____

_____

_____

_____

_____

_____

_____

_____

_____

_____

_____

_____

_____

_____

_____

_____

_____

_____

_____

_____

NOTES

*Uncommon Strategies for Making More Money
in 21st Century Food Service*